# Praise for *Kids Aren't Lazy*

"*Kids Aren't Lazy* is THE go-to book for parents and teachers of musicians of all ages. Everything in this book resonated with my journey as a mom of music students and as a teacher for many, many years of ages from 4 to 74. *Kids Aren't Lazy* is an exciting reference that I will be happy to require of all my students' parents and will use as a reminder for myself."

—*Kathleen Murphy Kemp*
*Assistant Professor of Orchestra Studies, Eastman School of Music*
*Assistant Principal Cello, Rochester Philharmonic Orchestra*
*Instructor of Cello and Chamber Music, Hochstein School of Music and Dance*

"In *Kids Aren't Lazy*, Haley's expertise in music performance and pedagogy shines brightly for fellow musicians, educators, and parents alike. One of the many significant achievements of this work is that the principles and values emphasized are not limited to the study and practice of music. It offers broad insight into any academic or artistic field."

—*Dr. Jungho Kim*
*Assistant Professor - Director of Orchestra and Conducting*
*Kent State University School of Music*

"Learning to play the violin is a metaphor for learning to deal with life. As Haley notes in *Kids Aren't Lazy*, the specific skills involved in playing a violin are representative of broader problem-solving tools and abilities necessary for a successful life. This information is what parents really want to know in order to help their children grow. I can think of no better path than participating with your child in the development of a skill and a discipline."

—*Charles L. Cox, Ph.D.*
*Clinical Psychologist*

"*Kids Aren't Lazy* helps the reader instill hope and confidence in children—our future. It provides directions and answers to anything we may face with our children and students in music and life—the ups, downs, detours, and celebrations. No issue has been left out. This book is a must-have for parents, teachers, musicians, and anyone interested in developing others to be their best."

—*Ben Ware*
*Director of Bands, Strake Jesuit College Preparatory*

"I cannot wait to share this with my own students' parents!"

—*Tara Fayazi*
*Music Teacher at Mannes Prep*
*Music Teacher at Education Through Music*

"Motivation can be difficult to address in weekly lessons and group classes. In *Kids Aren't Lazy*, Haley gives practical and loving advice to all who have experienced the joy and struggle of having a child study music. Haley assures the reader that parents and students are on a musical journey, and learning can be a roller coaster of success and disappointment at any stage.

As a violinist, teacher, and Suzuki parent, I highly recommend *Kids Aren't Lazy: Developing Motivation and Talent Through Music* as a comprehensive studio companion. It will be a valuable resource for myself and my studio parents."

—*Adrienne Caravan*
*Founder and Artistic Director, Sforza Suzuki String Program*

"A copy of this book will be in every one of my private studios."

—*Dominique McCormick*
*Founding Director, Century Fine Arts*

"Whether you are a teacher or a parent, you've got to read this book! With full awareness of the potential roadblocks in the shaping of a young musician, *Kids Aren't Lazy* provides strategies and new direction for all. Through Haley's very fine understanding of child, parent, and teacher psychology, she has put together a new paradigm that strengthens the routines and behavior of everyone involved. Her approach forms a team intent on success through joy, pleasure, comfort, respect, dedication, and positive reinforcement.

"*Kids Aren't Lazy* is a must-read for anyone involved in musical education."
—*Cécile Limon*
*Cardiff Violins*

"If you want to support your child's journey in music with a private teacher and participate in important and effective ways, this book clearly and convincingly explains, backed by thousands of hours of firsthand experience, the most successful ways to make that happen. *Kids Aren't Lazy* is a great addition to the literature."
—*Todd Frazier*
*Founder, American Festival for the Arts*
*Director, Center for Performing Arts Medicine at Houston Methodist Hospital*

"*Kids Aren't Lazy* is an invaluable resource for parents and teachers of young musicians. I highly recommend it to anyone interested in childhood music education."
—*Haley Moore*
*Music Educator (Violin), Louisiana State University*

"If investing in your child and their musical education is one of the best things you can do as a parent, reading *Kids Aren't Lazy* is the best way to prepare for your child's life-long journey into learning and falling in love with music. Anyone who seeks to create a happy, healthy learning environment for their growing musician should own a copy of this book!"
—*Karissa Chervnsik*
*Director of Orchestras, Baines Middle School*
*Violin Coach, Houston Youth Symphony*

# KIDS
## AREN'T
# LAZY

# *KIDS* AREN'T *LAZY*

## DEVELOPING MOTIVATION & TALENT THROUGH MUSIC

### LAUREN HALEY

PURPOSE
DRIVEN
PUBLISHING™

For permission requests, write to the publisher, addressed "Attention: Permissions Coordinator," at the address below.
Purpose Driven Publishing
141 Weston Street, #155
Hartford, CT, 06141

The opinions expressed by the Author are not necessarily those held by Purpose Driven Publishing.

Ordering Information: Quantity sales and special discounts are available on quantity purchases by corporations, associations, and others. For details, contact the publisher at the address above.

Edited by: Karen Ang
Cover design and photography: Albertine Wang
Violin: Thomas Smith. England, eighteenth century
Typeset by: Medlar Publishing Solutions Pvt Ltd., India
Printed in the United States of America.

ISBN: 978-1-946384-25-6 (print)
ISBN: 978-1-946384-26-3 (ebook)
Library of Congress Control Number: 2017963024

First edition, July 2018
The information contained within this book is strictly for informational purposes. The material may include information, products, or services by third parties. As such, the Author and Publisher do not aassume responsibility or liability for any third-party material or opinions. Readers are advised to do their own due diligence when it comes to making decisions.

*For Elvira "Forgie" Packer*

# Table of Contents

# Introduction

EVERYONE UNDERSTANDS THE desire to pursue a career out of a heartfelt passion. Music. Science. Football. I chose teaching because I passionately believe in people. And when you're looking for someone or something to believe in, there are no better people than children. Children are hope when the other things we love—music, science, football—become stale. This book is a heartfelt message to parents who believe in their kids just as passionately as I do.

No matter how much you love your career, parts of it will be unlikeable and uncomfortable. No matter how much you and your children love music and each other, parts of the journey will be difficult. You can demonstrate an unwavering belief in your child through this struggle and guide them through the inevitable difficulties in their pursuit of musical excellence.

As a teacher, I hear parents worry aloud that their child is musically broken—he's "lazy" and "unmotivated" or she's "just not talented." Sometimes rooted in this fear is the feeling that perhaps the parent has made mistakes in raising their child. Parents worry that they spend too much time at work. They worry that they themselves never attained musical proficiency, and therefore can't pass that magical "talent gene" to the next generation. Above all, parents feel guilt when the musical learning process proves more difficult than expected. How could something so positive as the study of music sometimes include genuinely painful learning experiences?

By contrast, it's been my experience that motivation and talent are not innate, fixed in place, or even the result of perfect parenting. Assuming that motivation and talent are gifts from birth or somehow baked-in is damaging to children and parents alike. Instead, let's define motivation as the learned rush of joy from overcoming past difficulties as one embarks on new tasks. Talent is the sum of these achievements that, put together, makes acquiring new skills easier. When understood this way, these gifts can be developed in anyone.

Parents who struggle at some point to get their children to practice are in the majority, not minority. Talent and motivation are not prerequisites to mastering "Twinkle, Twinkle, Little Star" or even Paganini's *24 Caprices*. Instead, the pursuit of excellence in music is a Trojan Horse; a vessel for the development of lifelong learning skills—persistence, critical thinking, discipline, and communication, just to name a few.

This book will help you to build your parent toolbox and to understand the nuanced yet crucial roles that creativity, fear, criticism, obstacles, and even failure play in your child's development. Together with your child's music teacher, you will discover how the pursuit of musical standards can drive the development of even more meaningful life learnings. Read on to discover effective strategies for developing your child's talent and motivation through the pursuit of musical achievement.

# Part 1
## Foster Motivation

# Chapter 1

## Show, Don't Tell

*"I tell her to practice, but she just never picks up the violin on her own."*
*"He doesn't respect the amount of money we spend on lessons."*
*"He never practices when we're home. It's like he's afraid of letting us see him actually try."*

LUDWIG VAN BEETHOVEN'S father, a raging alcoholic, dragged young Beethoven out of bed in the middle of the night to practice the piano. Antonín Dvořák's father pressured his son to become a butcher, not a composer. George Frideric Handel's father went so far as to forbid his son's musical practice. Despite the obstacles set out by their mostly well-intentioned parents, Ludwig, Antonín, and George left incredible legacies of disciplined and creative musical brilliance. Still, parent and teacher interactions with children undoubtedly shape growth and musical development. This chapter examines how our actions as parents and teachers can accelerate or stall the development of motivation and talent in young musicians.

Firstly, in our efforts to help children through the inevitable difficulties in music and school, we tend to provide exact solutions to problems, stifling natural opportunities to learn creative resolve through struggle. When we replace children's creative growth with our already-established abilities by overcoming obstacles on their behalf, we deny them the opportunity to realize the merit of their own ideas. In this situation, we unintentionally halt the development of motivation and talent.

Secondly, we turn children away from creativity by shaming them, through both words and actions. The parent who inhales sharply when a child tests a new passage on the violin and misses a note discourages the child from further trial and error on the instrument. Parental gestures like this make musical effort and growth unappealing. The child begins to think that violin—and art itself—should be beautiful (or at least easy) the first time around, with almost no process of development. This is problematic because everyone makes mistakes when developing skills, even when trying their best. There's an inherent learning curve to any pursuit. Moreover, music is challenging because its students perceive that everyone can hear and assess their journey through its early phases. Music's beginner stage can't be skipped, and overcoming it takes resilience, effort, and determination from the learner. Implying, even by accident, that a child's best effort is unsatisfactory inhibits their creativity and confidence before motivation and talent have had a fair chance to bloom.

The third, and ideal, course of action is to steer young artists toward creative development by helping them understand the intensive process that all works of art must undergo. Bearing this in mind, parents can positively guide children toward creativity by embracing the difficulties that artistic fields present. For example, when adults model productive behaviors in the face of musical challenges, they set the stage for the development of a child's creative work ethic. Consistently modeling the right behaviors shapes a home culture that demonstrates the value of artistic growth.

As a parent, you may have already noticed that telling someone to do something doesn't guarantee they will follow through. Telling your child to practice is about as effective as instructing your cat to please use the litter box. It may or may not actually happen, and your words won't have nearly as much impact as your actions. Effective practice happens as part of a daily habit, not an occasional (or even frequent!) verbal mandate. Coercing, coaxing, or bribing your child into practicing under supervision is ineffective and inefficient in the long run. Instead, read on to explore long-term methods for establishing a practice-friendly home and strategies for creating a culture for musical growth without resorting to repetitive words and instructions ("Have you practiced yet today?"). Given that effective role model behavior evolves based on your child's developmental stage, consult with your child's teachers on the specific behaviors they would like to see from you.

## Respect for Effort

It's always rewarding when parents positively affirm to their child a belief in their child's work. To supercharge this, show your child— through your own participation—the value of that work. There's a tendency to engage in positive spoken communication but remain unaware that silent or unintentional gestures can be powerfully destructive to the development of a child's motivation and talent. What child would want to practice if they believed their parents were dissatisfied with their accomplishments to date on their instrument?

The fundamental principle of a child's motivation to practice is the belief that something good will come from their work. If a young violinist is worried about their family overhearing wrong notes and reacting with laughter or disdain, they won't willingly touch the instrument. Children must have faith that they will accomplish something worthwhile when they choose practicing over another pastime. The establishment of that faith needs to start with you, the parent.

Parents commonly assume that their child shares their belief in their child's potential. In reality, young musicians worry that the world will discover they really are not as talented as their peers. Instead of assuming by default that they have limitless potential, children inherently fear that they genuinely lack talent. Young musicians are quite good at finding confirmation of this from friends, families, and teachers.

To demonstrate this distance between a parent's intent in coaching a child they believe in and their child's actual perception, let me tell you about a violin student named Britney. During Britney's violin lessons, her father, Jeff, sat nearby, listening to an audiobook as he typed on his laptop. Over his headphones, he could hear Britney play and would grimace and let out exasperated sighs of frustration at his daughter's attempts. Looking up periodically from his work, he would growl, "Come ON, Britney, you can do this!"

Jeff was delivering conflicting messages to Britney: his confidence that she should be able to accomplish the task at hand, but frustration and dismay with the results of her efforts. Further, although he had accompanied her to her lesson, not devoting his own attention to the process gave Britney the message that her lesson wasn't really a priority. Jeff's dismissal of Britney's many earnest tries made those attempts feel embarrassing, a process to be avoided instead of rewarded. His declaration that Britney could really accomplish this new technique made her feel like she was failing when she couldn't perform to his standards right then and there. While Jeff desperately attempted to affirm his belief in Britney's competence, the message as Britney perceived it instead confirmed her worst fears.

The first perspective to demonstrate if you want your child to embrace practicing is the idea that work is never wasted or done in vain. Acknowledge that (collectively) we are all afraid of barking up the wrong tree, spending time on something that's not worthwhile or that might make us look foolish. Your superpower, as a parent, is having the highest level of faith in your child's potential. Embrace this by showing up to lessons ready to notice and respect every small note, wrong or right. In doing so, you teach your child that these notes are worth their effort.

Next, remember that all of us (young and old) are hardwired to care about how others perceive us and our abilities. When children perceive that their work on an instrument brings them closer to their family and friends, they are more likely to pursue music wholeheartedly. Conversely, when young musicians fear that their work, effort, or results are laughable, foolish, or not appreciated, they tend to distance themselves from their instrument.

Finally, demonstrate to your child that trial and error is an integral part of music—and, in fact, every other worthy discipline. Affirm both verbally and through your own actions that you take your children's efforts seriously. Wrong notes are a crucial part of the creative process, no matter how hard one strives to avoid mistakes and cut them out of performances.

Have you ever built a LEGO house, only to have one of your children destroy it in a temper tantrum? Or submitted an idea to your boss only to have it coolly ignored or rejected? After such incidents, who doesn't feel disheartened? Similarly, when a young musician is told their practicing is painful to listen to (or when efforts are ignored altogether) they may wonder why they should bother. Yet, young musicians usually can't articulate this issue to family members. It's up to parents to understand that when children are too young to hear and appreciate their musical progress each day, their main reward for practicing is parental acknowledgment of effort and any newfound proficiency.

If a child secretly worries there is no hope for them musically, they have no self-directed reason to pursue further work on their instrument. If previous efforts were deemed unsatisfactory or irrelevant, it will be hard for the child to believe in the power of the same path today. If young musicians feel characterized as lazy or untalented after just a bit of learning, why should they throw more practicing into the ring? Many simply conclude that it's better to be characterized as lazy and escape into doing something else, like video games or TV.

You can show your child what's in your heart—hope for them to find fulfillment through music, to learn self-discipline, and to practice critical thinking on their instrument—by letting them see that you, too, progress via thoughtful trial and error, both at work and in your own creative pursuits.

When you even unintentionally condemn the results of a practice session rather than build on them, you destroy your child's musical LEGO house. Instead, demonstrate the utmost respect for your child's careful tries, including wrong notes. With this approach, your child will value their own persistence and effort even through complex tasks. This fundamental key to healthy self-esteem is the biggest building block for motivation.

---

Demonstrate the following principles to your child:

- Work is never done in vain. Even initial wrong answers are part of a work in process.
- Both easy and difficult tasks are worthy of respect.
- Regardless of age, genre, or level, honest musical work deserves respect.

---

## Encourage Curiosity

Each time a child experiences a new form of art, including music, they learn to respect the work of others, even if it's not to their own taste. Each new experience is a chance to fall in love with a new idea. Have you ever noticed how creative people always have room for one more passion or source of inspiration?

Surround your child with artistic role models by introducing them to everything from the Sistine Chapel to hand-painted wall signs. With free admission to many fine arts museums, youth orchestra concerts, library lectures, and local art festivals, a well-rounded arts education outside of school doesn't have to be expensive. Let your child see your enthusiasm for hearing a live performance or discovering a new artist. One day, your child will be the artist provoking these heartfelt reactions from audience members!

Teach your child how to listen to words, live music, and recordings, and to learn something of value from each work presented to them. Dismissing any form of art as too immature (cartoons), too highfalutin' (Impressionism), or too simple—I could have done that myself! (minimalism)—teaches young minds that certain types of art are of greater inherent value than others. It places artificial limits on the enjoyment of works, and puts children into a certain cultural box. By seeking diverse sources of inspiration, you give your child the chance to become a well-rounded artist.

Similarly, go out of your way to introduce your child to different genres of music. Even if you prefer Mozart, take the kids to a Beatles tribute concert. Listen to a percussion concerto if your child wants to be a violinist and visit an Impressionism exhibit even if you prefer Andy Warhol. Expand your child's tolerance for new experiences and teach them how to appreciate art in many forms. Art binds us together in humanity—it shows how people have always felt compelled to create meaningful work, regardless of their location, culture, or century. Curiosity about, tolerance for, and acceptance of new ideas, sounds, and experiences are key success factors. Demonstrate that no one type of art is inherently superior—human creativity comes in many forms.

## Respect for the Process

Do your best to uphold instructions from your child's private teacher. It may seem like music lessons are merely about improving on an instrument, but in addition to that, your child is picking up clues on adult responsibility from the way you work with their teacher. By following instructions on what to bring to class, for example, you show your child how directions from a teacher should be followed.

As a parent, you have the power to demonstrate an acceptance for academic and work-related processes in your home. Within this appreciation for persistence must come an acceptance of criticism. If you openly acknowledge the importance of healthy criticism to your own work, your child will understand its importance in theirs. For example, a child who cries when he has to play a musical passage more than once for a teacher is a child who believes he should never be criticized. Remedy this common roadblock by demonstrating a positive appreciation for feedback, including criticism. A healthy relationship with criticism is hugely beneficial to any child's future academic, athletic, and musical pursuits.

When most people think of intelligent students, they think of the kids who seem to always know all the right notes and answers. However, effective musical practice comes from generating learning procedures for finding new notes: it's not simply about recalling notes that have already been learned. In this way, music resembles math—teachers give students a mathematical method (long division, for example) and students learn by applying the method to new problems. Proficiency and confidence result from many applications of the method to solve different problems.

Look for ways to show your child how to harness both procedures and critical thinking to drive needed improvements. A classic approach to helping children learn how to solve math problems, for example, is to tell them to keep their pencils moving to avoid getting stuck. Music and math intimidate students when students try to find answers or notes out of thin air rather than through the learning procedure their teacher went over in class. When students do not immediately have an answer to a problem, they often assume failure. To remedy this, ask your child's teacher to help you apply appropriate procedures during your practice time with your child.

Another way to make learning palatable to children beginning an instrument is to try an instrument yourself as the parent. By taking the time to rent an instrument and bravely learning to play in the beginning, you show that you value the instrument as a challenge and know it can be conquered with work. Let your child see you put forth honest effort and still stumble over the same tricky musical passages they do. This helps them to not feel alone—you're in this together! It also helps you explain (to your child) how to do intricate technical moves on the instrument. If you can perform a musical task yourself, you can communicate more effectively to your child between lessons.

Music will inevitably involve struggles. In a two-parent household, make a pact with your partner to be a united model of resilience for your child. Parents can model calm behavior when children are upset by determining together how to react before these troubles occur. Agreeing beforehand on appropriate responses to tricky moments ("But, Daaaaad, I don't want to practice today! I hate violin!") makes it much more difficult for children to derail practice time.

Good role models stay the course and don't let predictable events (including frustrations or tantrums) distract them. For example, one rough lesson is temporary and will be forgotten in the grand scheme of things. Quitting an instrument in reaction to a lousy week would become a lifelong sore spot, verifiable proof in a child's belief that all along they really were just not talented.

Show appreciation for processes that are in the early stages. This is how great things start! "Lightly Row" played for the first time is every bit the miracle that your child's first Tchaikovsky performance will be. Enjoy each new accomplishment along the way and don't wait years to celebrate the milestones!

---

### Responsibility

Parents can demonstrate responsibility to young musicians by delivering on their own promises and being self-directed in fulfilling them. Look for opportunities to point out responsibilities in various areas of your life—work, personal, and fun. Let your child observe firsthand how professional, constructive relationships work. Narrate and explain your actions. Responsibility is a choice, and by showing your own decision-making, you give your child a voice of conscience to follow as they grow.

---

## Focus

Everyone knows that feeling of carrying work home from the office or always being on call. Music lessons present an opportunity to give your child all of your focus. Set the office work aside for another time. Show that few things are as important as your child's musical efforts. This has an added bonus for you, too: you'll come back to your deadlines with a fresh perspective after each musical break!

To maximize effective communication during lessons and direct your child's focus, demonstrate happy, attentive posture. The atmosphere in the lesson room changes when a child begins to struggle—kids shuffle their feet and look down, and often parental posture collapses. Reverse this mood by leaning in and engaging even more positively with the work to be done. Good posture and a smile translate into optimism. In this case, your optimism demonstrates support: you're proud of your child's work and happy to be on their team. By contrast, slouching back into the teacher's couch or staring down at papers, your phone, or a laptop isolates your child. It shows them they are in this lesson on their own.

Parents sometimes feel their child is too advanced for parental supervision in lessons to be helpful. Unsure that their presence adds value, they hesitate to attend classes. Plus, that childless hour seems perfect for a quick trip to the store or gym. Additionally, audiobooks are a tempting distraction for parents who stay through the lesson. As a teacher, let me be clear: No matter a child's age or musical ability, parental presence and focus in lessons always counts. It may seem reasonable to multitask (looking up from your phone at key moments, for example), but you will inevitably miss your child's nuanced improvements. More importantly, there is no one else whose reactions to particular triumphs or nuances in lessons matter more to your child than yours do. Young musicians may not be able to articulate how much your attention in lessons means to them, but they will appreciate your recognition as they progress in their studies.

Another strategy to build musical focus is to take detailed class notes in a dedicated lesson notebook. In doing so, you show your child that the information from their teacher is valuable and complex enough that it merits an effective record-keeping system. If a lesson concept seems too sophisticated or nuanced for parents to comprehend or record, why should a child feel full confidence in their ability to retain the information?

On a similar note, it's common for parents of beginners to bring only a tiny notebook to lessons. What message does this send? That music is a side subject; not serious enough to merit comprehensive note-taking. Instead, bring a full-sized, sturdy notebook and a pen. When you demonstrate seriousness and focus in ways like this, your child is more likely to follow suit. To really bring home the importance and privilege of lessons, videotape them (with teacher permission) via a smartphone or tablet.

## Emphasize Healthy Approaches

Never take away food or sleep as a punishment for setbacks or missed practice. On the flip side, avoid using food as a bribe for practicing or winning competitions. The promise of having steak for dinner tonight if the chair test is won will certainly not lead your child to greater self-propelled motivation, let alone a healthy relationship with food.

Elite performers make taking care of themselves and their instrument the highest priority. Effective teachers and parents show children how to treat their instruments and bodies with respect. All parties should emphasize daily practice over cram practice to prevent injury. Help your child prioritize their well-being by ensuring that they pace their work in a way that allows for a full night's sleep on a regular basis. Boom-and-bust practicing is tempting to procrastinators, but in reality, it is the fast track to injury. We'll talk more about how this happens in later chapters, but for now, understand that your child is closely observing your own relationship with work and health. They do not need to see you strike the perfect balance between work, family, and health, but they do need to observe that you value the effort it takes to care for oneself. Self-care is necessary for delivering the best possible work, and yet it's one of the first things neglected when assignments pile up.

## Aim for Consistent Progress

It's always difficult to get back to work on an instrument after a break (anything more than a day off from practice) as a natural result of lost muscle memory. Similarly, missing just one weekly lesson means fourteen days without teacher guidance, and at that next lesson, most children will find they have to completely repeat the previous lesson. Before casually cancelling lessons or practice sessions, ask yourself if it is worth the cost to your child's progress.

Balancing core subjects and other commitments with music is a common challenge. For example, when students miss lessons to prepare for exams, they quickly become overly discouraged by skill deterioration and foggy memories of the lesson material. Rather than confirming your child's fear that they can't handle both academics and music, help them build a daily agenda that provides for all learning activities. Stick with it even through difficult periods, like semester exams. This gives young musicians a repertoire of past triumphs to look back on the next time they feel overwhelmed! Remember, if it were truly impossible to balance music and academics, there would be no violin-playing pre-med students in prestigious universities. Instead, major cities throughout the United States have well-established doctors' orchestras for exactly this type of musician.

Show your child their music lessons are a priority by committing to show up each week on time. Habitual lesson cancellations and tardiness send the message that other areas of your life take precedence. If you wouldn't want your child to look for excuses to skip practicing, don't let cancelled lessons set that tone. Emergencies will happen, but predictable events (a birthday party, guests in town, substantial homework) shouldn't disrupt your child's lesson routine.

## Respect Mentors

Young musicians can demonstrate respect for their teacher—and for the privilege of working one-on-one with an artist—by dressing appropriately for lessons. Clothing should be in good repair, and children should come to lessons with their hands washed. This isn't about the teacher: most do not care at all how students dress. Instead, this is a way of helping children learn the appropriate level of respect required when working closely with mentors. When adults set these social boundaries (starting with appropriate dress and grooming), children learn that investing in relationships with others reflects an investment in themselves.

While everyone loves the teacher who goes by their first name—Mr. Joe, Ms. Jane—students who address teachers by last names tend to regard those teachers with more authority. This carries over to responsiveness regarding assigned deadlines and practice resolutions. Even though you as the parent may be on first-name terms with your child's teacher, always use formal names (Mr. Johnson, Ms. Smith) whenever your child is in the room, even at home. Most importantly, avoid trash-talking your child's teacher. Take appropriate action to resolve issues as necessary, but keep any disputes private to avoid distracting your child.

Consider the way your interactions with teachers frame your child's perspective on appropriate behavior for working relationships. Even if you consider yourself to be a close friend of your family's private music teacher, the boss-employee relationship is still there. Think of the following topics as off-limits during lessons: politics, religion, your teacher's personal life, money or finances, disparaging remarks with regard to ethnicity, foul language, any bathroom references (TMI! Also, in the case of your child, not yours to share!), gossip about other teachers or students, and bad-mouthing your spouse or child. If you wouldn't discuss these non-music topics with your boss or employees, they shouldn't be brought up in lessons, either. Your teacher may react professionally in these conversations, but they may feel they have no choice other than to smile and nod.

Effective relationships take work, and curating appropriate conversations is part of that work. Establishing deliberate conversational boundaries keeps lessons efficient (and on-track) and sets your child up for better teacher-student and employee-employer relationships in the future.

Finally, demonstrate respect for teachers by paying tuition on time. When children see parents neglect to pay tuition, they may be embarrassed or, alternatively, may question if their lessons have real value. Show that classes are important by talking to your child about how tuition is a demonstration of your belief in their future. Discuss what it means to invest in learning, and how they can fulfill this investment by practicing.

---

### A Note on Parent-Free Lessons

Some teachers prefer for parents to not attend lessons. The general thought is that this allows kids to feel freer with their teacher, and to be more emotionally expressive in their music than they would be if their parents were there. Many professionals strongly condemn this approach. It's best for children to first learn to play bravely in front of their parents before they perform for larger audiences. Think carefully about the seriousness of a teacher who dismisses the role of parents so casually. The benefits to any child's education from having close parental involvement far outpace any detraction.

---

## Let Your Guard Down

In the race to be the best version of ourselves for children and friends, adults often shy away from admitting personal flaws. We claim all the typical excuses for failed resolutions ("It's just a stressful time at work right now.") and in social media paint a picture for others that's more ideal than daily reality. Similarly, many parents figure that the more perfect they appear to their children, the more effective their parenting efforts will be.

While it's true we should always strive to be our best selves, some of the most effective mentoring happens when we, as parents, educators, and artists, let our guard down and admit our shared difficulties. By humanizing ourselves and the struggles we all face, we demonstrate to young musicians that it's okay to battle through challenges. We show young musicians how to persevere, rather than give up, after experiencing a loss or failure.

One of the most effective learning moments of my performance career was the worst audition I have ever done. I completely failed to control my nerves: I just fell apart on stage. The audition went so poorly that I arranged a meeting with the conductor (who heard my audition) the following week to regroup about what had happened. To my surprise, he shared with me that he had faced similar struggles as a young musician. He told me, "I'm no stranger to these kinds of [anxiety] attacks. I found that when I turned around and faced the orchestra [as the conductor instead of as an instrumentalist], I could put the audience behind me."

Despite the orchestra's cutthroat, admit-no-weaknesses culture that so valued perfection, our revered conductor was admitting a personal weakness. Understanding that this musical titan had overcome the same struggle as me and had grown to become so widely acclaimed inspired me. His talent was created through difficulty and struggle; it was not born as a gift from the universe. Through his frankness in sharing his own story with me, I gained more respect for him than in any other moment of my training. Even better, his story gave me reason to believe in my own musical future.

## Silent Destructive Behaviors

As you see, parents can facilitate positive learning outcomes through silent actions as well as through spoken support. The flip side of this power is that it's possible to be unintentionally destructive in the same way. These behaviors may go virtually unnoticed by us as adults but can be crushing to the young musicians we so aim to inspire. This behavior is analogous to an *own goal* in hockey—accidentally tipping the puck into your own team's net, scoring a point for the opposing team.

Usually, these own goals happen as an outlet for our own frustration as parents and educators—we scoff at a child's missed note that seems too trivial to be happening incorrectly *yet again*. We laugh a little too hard at a child's serious attempt, and they perceive our laughter as being directed at them rather than with them. In an attempt to keep our busy worlds running, we text during children's music lessons, silently demonstrating that this kid stuff can't be the focus of our world for a single hour. Worse, we joke with children that we still love them even though they made a mistake in the recital.

The pattern here is that own goals happen when adults belittle the seriousness in a child's heart. It's so easy to forget that children are constantly listening for the approval of the adults in their lives. As a result, we unintentionally sabotage efforts, dampening motivation before talent even has a chance to develop.

Instead, let's look for creative ways to give even the smallest child's spark of confidence a platform. Kids are looking for reasons to believe in themselves while simultaneously waiting for confirmation that they really are no good after all. Let's have even our silent actions back up the motivation in young musicians' hearts. Let's give them every reason to believe that good things will happen if they persevere.

Scoffs, winces, disappointed faces—all of these wordless actions can paralyze a child with anxiety or embarrassment. What could be more discouraging to a child than perceiving that their parents think of them as foolish or unsuccessful? Kids aren't usually self-aware enough to articulate this fear and their resulting reluctance to play or perform is often blamed on shyness. Adults unintentionally make these feelings worse by drawing attention to the awkward and disheartening squeaks that instruments make in the beginning of anyone's study. Gasping at any sound is disruptive and destructive. Your child's teacher has fixed these squeaks and wrong notes from little ones and their instruments for years. Let them help you call attention to these issues in the most productive way.

# Chapter 2

---

# Shape Success Through Routines

*"Sure, he listens to his teacher, but he doesn't listen to me. I'm so, so sick of fighting with him over violin. If he fails, it's his own fault—I told him what he needed to do ten times. I even call him from work to see if he's practicing! He could be so good at the violin, but he's just too lazy."*

AT ONE TIME or another, absolutely every music student clashes with their parents over practicing. No matter how much your child loves music, this hiccup *will* happen. If we, as parents and teachers, believe we should never struggle with getting our young musicians to practice, our frequent conclusion when we do experience that conflict is that the child is just lazy or unmotivated. However, no matter how high a child's perceived energy level or interest in music is, they will eventually need guidance on how to move forward when practice motivation stalls.

Despite how common this problem is, it's a deciding factor when children quit lessons. Parents decide music is simply not worth the strife at home, especially because this refusal to practice often looks like genuine disdain for the instrument. Add to this the cost and logistics of getting to regular lessons, and many busy adults will decide that the musical return on their investment is simply not there. However, building a positive home practice culture—where daily musical work happens as a rule, not an exception—is in your reach.

## Maria's Story

Maria was one of my first students. She came to lessons with her tiny violin and her Suzuki books, dressed in glittery T-shirts and a messy ponytail, like so many six-year-old girls. Maria's father, Matthew, saw Maria's musical potential but didn't seem to see her age. If Maria didn't perform well in class, Matthew would look over to me and say, "It's not that she's not smart, it's that Maria is lazy."

When Maria struggled with a new technique, even something we had only just started learning, Matthew would blame her struggle on the previous week's practice (or lack thereof), repeating what soon became a weekly refrain: "Maria is lazy. She doesn't want to practice. She only wants to watch TV. I call her, every night, on my way home from work and ask her to practice, and she still doesn't do it."

When I asked Matthew if Maria's mother, Diane, could help Maria practice, Matthew insisted Diane knew nothing about violin and she didn't want to "mess up" Maria's efforts. Matthew felt he wasn't able to help Maria because it was usually Maria's bedtime before he even got home.

It became clear to me that Maria's routine—of coming home from school, practicing alone, and going to sleep before her "violin parent" arrived home from work—was causing a huge slowdown for her musical progress. Even worse, every time Maria came to a lesson, she heard "Maria is lazy." What child would want to pursue an instrument when it's the source of such isolation at home and reprimand during lessons? Something had to be done before Maria truly began to internalize the mindset of "Maria is lazy."

I brought up these issues with Maria's parents. To begin, Maria, at the age of six, certainly needed supervision during practice. While that seemed obvious to me as a teacher, it took a while for Matthew to understand that he couldn't expect Maria to make measurable progress on her own at home—even if Maria had played well in her lesson that week. Our second problem was scheduling. We either had to find a way for Maria to still be awake when her father came home so the two could work together or we had to give Diane more musical support, especially given that she was unable to attend Maria's lessons.

In this case, technology came to our rescue. We started videotaping Maria's lessons so Diane could watch them with Maria before the two started practicing together. Recording our lessons motivated Maria to practice more at home—she wanted to play well for the camera! Moreover, having the resource of lesson videos made Diane feel more confident that her guidance during Maria's practice sessions would be worthwhile and effective.

Instead of preferring mindless, solitary activities (iPad games, TV) at the end of each day—activities that didn't lead to concrete skill improvement or recognition from her parents—Maria looked forward to working with her mother each evening. Maria loved this special Maria and Mom Time. As a bonus, because her practice sessions were so much more effective than they had been when she practiced alone, Maria gained confidence in her playing.

This quick progress motivated Maria, and she began to ask to practice every day after school. Diane excitedly shared with me that Maria had even awakened her parents early one morning asking if they could all work on violin together before school.

With routine working for their family, rather than against them, Maria, Diane, and Matthew found joy in their pursuit of music. Even better, Matthew stopped repeating, "Maria is lazy." He understood that with situation modification, Maria genuinely enjoyed practicing.

## Creating a Routine

### Build on Current Structures

If your child always brushes their teeth at 6:50 a.m. before leaving for school, add five minutes of practicing at 6:55 a.m. Another good time is immediately following the after-school snack most children have. Finishing the snack is the cue to practice. In this way, you can hook practicing onto a routine that is already well established. Disregard potential cues that your child still struggles with—practicing after math homework won't work if your child struggles to start math assignments before 9 p.m. Additionally, avoid cutting fun activities short to fit the new practice routine into your child's life. No child will respond positively to turning off their favorite TV show each evening to accommodate musical study.

### Work with, Rather than Against, the Desire to be Social

Avoid causing your child to leave a group activity, like breakfast with family, for solo practicing. Rather than letting the rest of the household watch a movie while one child practices, have everyone pursue equally productive tasks. Otherwise, you will create the impression of unfairness. Would you feel more attached to your work if you missed a family outing to finish it? Most likely not. If a child is old enough to practice effectively alone, but still falls prey to distractions, it can be helpful for one parent to sit silently on the couch (perhaps reading a book) during practice. This silent company helps children to focus on their goals rather than on the feeling of isolation as they work.

## Start Small

As the parent, your task is to facilitate ease in the establishment of a practice routine. Tackling too much too soon is why new routines fail after the first week. Make the goal to simply get the instrument out of the case at the same time every day. This may feel too slow, and perhaps not even worth doing, but the mission here is to *develop a routine, not the notes*. Resist the temptation to add excessive content-based practicing with your child just to capitalize on the first few days of success. When your child wants more time with the instrument at the end of a mini practice session, they experience an early spark of motivation!

## Agree on a Way to Let Your Child be Self-directed

Develop self-direction by using phone alarms and timers (instead of verbal reminders) to cue the start of practice sessions. Agree with your child to set matching alarms on your phones. Then, simply meet in the same room to practice when the alarms go off. Beware of the pitfall of having just a little bit of your own work to finish when you should be ready to practice with your child. Consider setting an additional alarm for yourself a few minutes before each practice session: this will help transition your focus to the musical work at hand after your other daily tasks.

## Troubleshooting & the Chief Practicing Engineer

Think of yourself as the Chief Practicing Engineer (CPE), ready to solve problems that might get in the way of practicing. Avoid unintentionally creating situations where your child might feel forced to choose between practicing and any other activity, whether academic, leisure, or social. Some parents fear that if they set a rigid practice schedule for their child they lose the chance to allow the child to be self-directed. I argue instead that parents must first demonstrate successful routines and only then should a child be given the option of deciding when to practice each day. This strategy has the further benefit of endowing young learners with time management skills as their academic careers become more demanding.

Creating a daily routine is challenging for parents. Naturally, as a side effect, some desired activities have to be deferred for the prioritized ones to benefit. A crucial part of the CPE's task is to resist the temptation to scrap the routine on some days to fit in an additional activity. For example, soccer may have to wait one season until a more convenient game schedule is available. This season, perhaps baseball fits better.

Additionally, beware of pop-up events that challenge practice time. When you choose a one-off activity over practicing, you unintentionally create a hierarchy of importance in your child's mind. Instead, strive to balance music with other activities. Should something truly spectacular create a conflict, brainstorm a plan with your child to make the day's practice happen. Discussing the importance of routine and jointly deciding on a contingency plan—for emergency use only—helps children feel responsible for their own schedule. This strategy develops accountability, which will serve children well as they mature.

As with all potential obstacles, make a plan for your child's objectives ahead of time and discuss expectations together. Then stick with the plan. If the plan is for your child to practice while Grandma and Grandpa take the dogs for a walk, follow through on that plan. Don't let Grandma and Grandpa decide to watch a movie with the other siblings and still expect your child to choose practicing over social time. That would demonstrate failure on your part of the bargain and you would be asking your child to choose between time with family and keeping their promise to practice.

As the CPE, establishing a practice routine in your schedule exemplifies that music takes priority and is a fixture in your child's life. Should a major long-term conflict present itself, write a substitute practice time (as close to the usual time as possible) into your family's calendar for the relevant days or weeks. Anticipating schedule conflicts prevents unintentional derailments.

Pursuing a diverse range of extracurricular activities helps children become well-rounded, but music as a long-term pursuit requires constant prioritization to facilitate proficiency on any instrument. Remember: an activities list that prioritizes every possible extracurricular effectively prioritizes no particular pursuit. *For your child to stand out musically, music must stand out in your child's list of priorities.*

## Strategic Scheduling

Think of your child's most productive moments. What time each day is your child usually at his or her best? For example, practicing in the morning is usually ideal for the littlest musicians (ages five and under). Avoid anything close to nap time (before or after). Close the doors to the practice room and make sure the rest of the family knows that practicing is special time for you and your young musician. If your spouse or another adult is home, delegate all other parenting responsibilities to them for a few minutes. Hand over your cell phone and turn off anything noisy. Put the pets in another room. It is often more challenging to carve out a few minutes of quiet time like this than it is to actually practice.

Practicing before school is initially challenging for some families, but it is by far the best for developing a sense of accomplishment (and therefore self-esteem) in young musicians. While evening practice forces students to balance homework, family time, and practicing (along with the guilt that comes when they skip one of the three!), morning practice gives children a positive achievement with which to start their day. Few children are naturally "morning people" through high school, but you can help them take on morning productivity and its rewards with the hope that it will serve them well throughout their lives.

When children, regardless of age, feel they have already made a great decision for the day, they view themselves positively and continue to make equally wise moves regarding their schoolwork. In so doing, they also learn that the purpose of punctuality with regard to practicing and school assignments is to complete work before negative feelings (like dread and procrastination) creep in.

## Identifying Responsibilities

*"I call Stacy every day on my way home to work to tell her to practice, but she just does not listen to me!"*
*"Mom, I was practicing. It's just that Tom kept interrupting me and I had too much homework to keep playing!"*

You would be hard-pressed to find a family that couldn't relate to these exchanges! Everyone wants to make the best possible impression on their teacher, and it's common for parents and children to throw each other under the bus in lessons to avoid embarrassment over a lack of practicing. Take comfort in the fact that the prevalence of this issue makes it a worthy task for teachers and parents.

First, know that teachers aren't interested in assigning blame for a rough week of practicing. They understand that it's not a flaw to struggle and everyone has to deal with the learning curve of developing a practice time routine. Their opinion of you will not suffer when you admit that both you and your child are works in progress. As people, we are all in a position to strive for better daily efforts and results.

Parents and teachers can set constructive examples by acknowledging places where they, too, have struggled. Presented with positive examples of upward striving, young musicians become more willing to try openly. Similarly, when adults are upfront and realistic about a particular week's obstacles, children tend to be as well. Don't worry that kids need a perfect parental example to be able to follow through on their own tasks. Instead, show how you confront difficulties and how you set out to solve them. Let your child see you work.

Teachers want to work with you and your child as a team to confront challenges together. As the parent, you may feel that you or your child made mistakes in trying to practice this week. We can all relate to the feeling that if only we had been a better person/ parent/child, things would have gone better! There's also the mindset of, "Surely next week, when science club is over, we will finally achieve the perfect violin practice week." Teachers, however, are truly uninterested in this game. All they want is to help your family move forward. They will be excited to hear about every new challenge your family confronts as the days go by.

To help minimize strife and the blame game as it pertains to each week's musical work, agree with your child and teacher ahead of time about each other's responsibilities when it comes to practicing. Openly discussing these responsibilities sets appropriate expectations. Clear expectations provide a solid base for routines and goals. Establishing guidelines like this teaches your child how open and healthy collaboration leads to positive and successful outcomes for all.

Lastly, consider how you might allow your older child to self-regulate while sticking to their practice schedule. If the minute they leave the practice room to get a drink, you bark, "Get back in that room and finish your practicing!" they will feel shame and want to distance themselves from the instrument and you. True, children may use, "I'm thirstyyyy," as an excuse to get out of practicing for a few minutes, but as they mature they will learn to take healthy breaks as their focus allows.

---

### Responsibility Agreements

**Teacher**
- Helps students and parents identify goals
- Prompts families to brainstorm solutions to obstacles

**Parents**
- Provide a safe and quiet practice environment
- Maintain the instrument

**Child**
- Brings problems to the attention of teacher and parents
- Follows through with practicing agreements
- Engages with the trial and error process

---

## Keeping Routines Through Breaks and Holidays

Present your child with video interviews of artists and athletes. You won't need to point out to your child that dancers practice every day, even on Christmas, if those artists do the explaining for you. If you tell your child, "Yo-Yo Ma practiced his cello on holidays as a child!" the implication is that you wished your child had the same inclination as Yo-Yo Ma—a completely different human being about whom they know relatively little. Your child, potentially preferring to participate in special once-a-year activities instead of setting aside time to practice, will feel inferior to Yo-Yo Ma. That's counterproductive. Instead, simply let your child draw their own conclusions about how high-achievers practice by providing access to books and movies about these artists. Exposure to stellar role models is highly motivating, and children feel proud imitating the dedication they see from professionals.

Be aware that vacations can massively derail musical momentum. Talk beforehand to set expectations—is the instrument coming along on the trip? If so, when and where will practice take place? If the instrument must be left at home, when will your child confront the missed work after the trip?

Speak with your family's teacher about strategies for extended trips. If multiple lessons will be missed, your teacher may be able to provide appropriate goals, strategies, and feedback while you are away. Because the practice of making music is physical, mental, and highly nuanced, muscle memory and skill fade every day that the instrument remains untouched in its case. There is no such thing as maintaining proficiency without consistent practice.

For this reason, many serious teachers will not retain students who do not study their instrument during the summer. While summer breaks may be the cultural norm for schools, teachers and players notice that these breaks cause severe skill deterioration. As an exciting alternative, use breaks for accelerated musical learning (through lessons, music festivals, workshops, and daily practice) so your child resumes school recharged and ready for new challenges.

## Pitfalls

There will always be justifiable excuses to ditch practice, exercise, or diet regimes on a given day. The best strategy here is to stick with daily routines no matter what else comes up. For example, when conflicts inevitably arise, simply repeat, "Whether it's Tuesday, Friday, or Sunday, we always practice together after breakfast." This shows your child that nothing dislodges practice—instead, other things are moved to accommodate practice.

When parents condone missed practice, children hunt for other seemingly valid excuses. To remedy this, agree with any other adults at home on what constitutes a bona fide excuse (true emergencies) to skip practicing. Then stick to that standard. In difficult situations, recognize that routines bring comfort to children. Coming back to the routine is a healthy way to deal with reality after an unusual or disruptive event.

It will always be more difficult for you as the adult to make time in your life for a practicing routine than it will be for your child to do the same. That's okay; you're ready for it. Your child has never pursued a routine like this before and they are just trying it on for size. Be willing to wrestle with this new plan together. Above all, make sure you're not the first to break from it. Doing so would demonstrate a low excuse threshold to your child. You don't want to convey that the next get-out-of-practice excuse is just around the corner. Instead, teach that excuses may be tempting, but your child doesn't need to give in to them.

It's a guarantee that life will give you a reason to skip practice every day for the first few weeks of any routine. This isn't your fault, it's just reality. Start with the smallest possible dose of practice and celebrate that you and your child made it through this initial challenge. You don't need to pretend to be completely motivated and ready to work all the time. You just need to pursue the routine again and again each time the calendar throws a curveball.

Don't worry about matching the practice routine of older or more advanced players. Let their success be joyful and motivating, but avoid pointing out to your child how others are "better" at practicing. **Children become what you tell them they are, so as teachers and parents, we should never tell a child they are lazy or imply that they are inferior in any way to other kids.** Let's tell them instead that their journey is just beginning. They will grow into advanced players one day at a time.

Practice is work. Work is required no matter what subject or career one pursues. The expectation that children should *always* love violin and *always* want to play is damaging. Of *course* parents are distressed when a child confesses that he doesn't enjoy practicing—instruments and lessons consume huge parental resources and energy, after all! This declaration—"Mom, I hate practicing"—leads parents to believe they should let their children quit music. Not to worry: Everyone—everyone!—who performs professionally wanted to quit at one time or another growing up. Your reaction to this phase will shape the way your child deals with future obstacles. Simply remind your child that sometimes work is fun and sometimes work is work, and the pursuit of music is a great example of this. Choosing routine over excuses will become a powerful path to resilience and coping skills for your family.

Routines require a tremendous emotional and time-based investment from parents, especially in the beginning. If parents aren't willing to invest their time in establishing a daily practice routine, why should children bother to practice an instrument that squeaks for the first year?

## Mental Distractions

Everyone loves anticipation. When special occasions, like birthdays, holidays, and sporting events, are imminent, it's tough for young musicians to fully engage with their practice content. Haven't you ever felt that you just could not wait to finish your work at the office so you could attend a friend's celebration?

Children are so much like adults in this way. If you set up the party streamers while your child practices, they will perceive that they are missing out on the joyful anticipation and preparation. Agree with your child that you will both focus on work at the same time so you can prepare for and celebrate the special occasion later that day together.

## Material Distractions

Uh oh: Your child has a brand-new toy and just can't wait to play with it. You know that letting them play now will leave them with less focus for their practice later in the day, if it even happens at all. On the other hand, if you force them to practice now, time will crawl by until they can play with their toy! Neither option will lead to an increased affection for music. To avoid conflict, it may seem like allowing your child to play with their toy before practice would be okay, just this once. By contrast—this situation presents the opportunity to create a positive learning experience using the practice timer.

Strike a deal with your child to alternate between a given amount of practice time and toy time. For example, set a timer for fifteen minutes of practice time and then again for fifteen minutes of toy time. Agree that neither of you will try to extend either activity. Be aware that even when your child has put the toy down, their thoughts might drift back toward it. That's okay—this experience teaches children how to balance excitement and work.

---

### Tips for the "Other" Parent

*"Practicing is his mother's field, I know nothing about violin."*
*"Mom, Dad said I didn't have to practice today because my science project is due!"*

When children see a crack in the parent-parent practice strategy, they take advantage of it, no matter how self-motivated they are. Strategize with your partner to enforce consistent standards and avoid creating conflicts.

---

## Key Phrases

Kids are experts at wiggling out of commitments. Don't give them a chance to advocate for skipping the day's practice session. Rather than engaging them in a battle of wits (as the clock runs out), simply repeat the following phrases:

*We always practice at 5 p.m.*
*We can talk about it later, but for now we're sticking to The Plan.*
*Sometimes practicing is easy, sometimes it's not.*
*We're still going to do it.*

You don't need to provide any other rationale. Repeating neutral words back to your child (no matter what new arguments they present) de-escalates the conversation. Plus, this broken record strategy allows you to retain your composure and your power over the situation. With a shrug, you put up a wall to arguments and excuses: "We always practice at 5 p.m., end of story." Avoid raising your voice or overemphasizing words (*We ALWAYS practice at 5 p.m.!*). Calmly state the fact. Children quickly figure out that it's easier to just practice than it is to argue with a "robot voice."

## Difficult Situations

### Divorce or Separation

As a teacher, I see how much more difficult maintaining a musical routine is for parents who are raising a child in two homes. It's hard enough for cohabiting parents to exercise consistent discipline together. If this situation fits you, take heart: you are absolutely not alone in facing these difficulties. Talk to your child's teacher about how other families in the studio have handled this journey. Teachers see this frequently and can offer tips for efficient practice routines and behaviors when children split their time between houses.

### Moving

After a move, some young musicians absolutely refuse to touch their instrument, no matter how much they loved it in their old town. It reminds them of their friends, teachers, and old routine. Most children willingly return to music when they're less emotional. However, lost muscle memory after time away from the instrument is a frustrating surprise when playing is resumed. To ease this transition, don't wait for your child to pick the instrument up again naturally before you decide to find a new teacher. Ideally, contact potential teachers before the move: many in-demand teachers will have a waiting list.

### Disruptive Behavior

What about when a child cries? What if they declare, "It's not fair!" and then throw the instrument on the floor? Bad behavior happens to good kids, especially when they're little. If you (unintentionally) demonstrate that bad behavior upsets you (and can therefore end the practice session), your child will bring out the tears again the next time they feel stuck. It's a sneaky way to end work. Instead of getting upset, acknowledge that good kids do bad things. Resolve to react calmly and consistently. Little outbursts shouldn't derail the routine.

# Chapter 3

---

# Harness Criticism
# to Build Self-Esteem

*"I'm just trying to help, but practicing always ends in a fight.
I tell her to be picky and pay attention to the details, but she
just plays too fast to get anything done!"*

MUSICAL PERFORMANCE BENEFITS from the relentless pursuit of ever higher standards. As adults, we recognize that receiving constructive feedback is crucial to success in almost any professional career. Similarly, we recognize that when we provide guidance throughout a child's practice sessions, we help them develop persistence, reflection, and self-direction.

However, delivering constructive criticism to advance musical technique is neither intuitive nor easy. You can advance your ability to provide this guidance: it starts with nuanced attention to the well-being of your parent-child relationship at every moment during practice. Providing appropriate feedback—even through difficult moments—is an investment in your child's learning skills and in their future ability to accept meaningful critique.

Effective criticism, at its heart, is about empowering children to build learning processes. When you demonstrate how to approach musical or technical obstacles, you teach your child how to reflect on their playing and also how to tackle future challenges, including academic pursuits. Ask yourself, "How do I want my children to judge their own work when they're older? Do I want them to be sweeping, vague, or negative? Do I want them to be steady, consistent, picky, and positive?" Frequently, the way we, as adults, criticize ourselves and others fails to model the constructive and positive criticism behaviors we would like to develop in young musicians.

The goal for criticism is simple: Teach students (of any subject) to keep their pencils moving, practice honest reflection, generate solutions, and strive for higher standards. To put this mathematically: *improvement* is the constant in your child's practicing equation each day. The variable is whatever current challenge they face.

Appropriate criticism empowers young musicians. Inappropriate criticism empowers doubt. Positive criticism builds new structures onto existing efforts. Destructive criticism tears down what has already been built. Where proper guidance builds skills, ineffective criticism at best maintains the status quo or worse, damages a child's belief in their own potential.

While some level of conflict and frustration is inevitable over the years as your child pursues an instrument (just ask any musician, parent, or teacher!), successful practice with your child will hinge on your style of communication. In this chapter, we will explore strategies for harnessing the power of criticism, navigating musical challenges, and raising any child's ability to self-direct.

## Build Closeness

Why is investing in parent-child musical learning worth the struggle? What does it do for your child's emotional and academic growth? What does it do for your relationship with your child as they grow?

The fundamental principle in using criticism to build your child's self-esteem is to recognize that your criticism must always be demonstrably from a place of unconditional respect and love. This must be made clear to your child at absolutely every stage—it truly bears repeating as a family principle. Children must never, ever feel that parental love hinges on performance. Show them that because you love them unconditionally you will be there to help them face every musical and academic obstacle. In doing so, you prepare them to conquer future life obstacles as well. To many parents, this love seems so obvious, but students confess to teachers that they worry about losing parental affection when they miss notes. When children feel this way, it becomes difficult for them to truly enjoy studying music.

## Hope Matters

To put in anything more than a half-hearted effort, your child must believe from the bottom of their heart that their musical work will pay off. Who would want to practice if they viewed lessons as an endless stream of criticism instead of as an unlimited source of improvement? What child would willingly pick up their instrument if they believed that their family, friends, or teachers considered them to be musically inadequate?

Young musicians usually aren't able to articulate their fear of being less talented than others. They see other musicians effortlessly perform "finished" works and don't witness the effort it took to build that musical skill. Parents and teachers hear and see moments of musical progress, but the child struggling over technique often does not. This makes it easy for children to become discouraged: "Everyone else seems to perform effortlessly, so why is the violin so difficult for me? I feel like there are always mistakes!" Parents and educators can remedy this by showing children how impressive feats onstage are exclusively the result of the persistence and attention to detail that children are developing at home.

The development of persistence and attention to detail is the true aim for all effective criticism. Avoid statements that imply backward growth ("You fixed that last week—why is it out of tune again today?!") or a lack of natural ability—these destroy your child's faith in their own ability to improve.

When children believe that they will noticeably improve when they follow their practice plans, they view practicing as a worthy investment. Practicing becomes satisfying, rewarding, and fun instead of mandated, pointless, or depressing. When guiding your child's practice, make sure their confidence in their own development remains intact, even through your pickiest moments.

To illustrate this point, let me tell you about one of my students, Michelle. When we first started lessons, Michelle was a struggling beginner, self-conscious about every note. She barely let her bow touch the strings, and as a result, the higher strings on the violin squeaked and the lower ones only emitted unattractive growls. In one lesson, Michelle's mother, Miriam, laughed and pointed out that the lower strings sounded like farts when Michelle played. Miriam meant this comment in good humor, but Michelle was mortified.

Miriam and I spoke after the lesson about how a comment that seems harmless (to a parent) can make a child feel self-conscious or untalented. For Michelle to overcome her fear of sounding bad (which, of course, was physically causing her violin to squeak!), Michelle needed more confidence in her own potential. This meant that Miriam would have to find ways to demonstrate her belief in

Michelle's potential and avoid any humorous comments at Michelle's expense. Three years later, I'm happy to report that Michelle confidently and beautifully performs in public, and her family proudly recognizes her musicality and perseverance.

As we explore this, remember that you, as a parent, don't need a project to start out perfect or even dignified to have confidence in it. Look for ways to show your child how things are built—a house under construction is always an aesthetic nightmare, but the final product is beautiful. More often than not, one must go through a messy phase (squeaky notes included) to create beauty.

## Know What You're Really Building

Emphasize criticism as a journey, not just as a means to an end. This will help your child realize that working together brings you joy—you don't require perfection to feel proud, you just want to witness honest effort. Valuing effort over perfection isn't the same as settling for mediocrity—instead, it's merely an acknowledgment that the journey for self-improvement is endless. Upholding a picky, persistent process is far more important than arbitrary perfection on a single note.

With this mindset, you can develop healthy self-improvement and self-esteem patterns in your child as they grow. This open communication, paired with constantly visible respect, patience, and love, is a wonderful investment in your parent-child relationship!

## Employ Guiding Questions

Something sounds terrible. You know the teacher wanted it fixed, and yet you find that you can't specifically spell out for your child how to solve this particular musical passage. Not to worry, you are far from the only parent with this particular problem! There's actually a huge learning opportunity here: rather than fixing specific notes (teachers call this spoon-feeding), you have the chance to teach your child how to generate their own solutions.

To achieve this, ask your child's teacher for some general questions to pose during practice. We'll call these Guiding Questions. You may not know the answer to these questions yourself for every musical passage in a piece, but your prompt will push your child in the right direction. As a teacher, I find that young musicians usually know how to solve problems as they practice but have trouble identifying specific actions to try without such prompts.

Examples of Guiding Questions include, "What do you think about that note?" and "Could you play that for me again, but more slowly?" Teaching through questions is more effective than teaching through statements because it guides children through a learning process, generating far more talent development than rote learning or memorization do. Additionally, kids prefer processes to rote learning (or worse, spoon-fed answers) because this style of learning is more engaging—a hunt for the answer is always fun! Most importantly, when children solve their musical dilemma (a squeak, an out of tune note) on their own with just a small clue, they feel competent and productive. These feelings spur self-direction, focus, and motivation.

Children often feel overwhelmed with content ("I'll never get this whole page right!") when they are really just stuck on what to fix next. Children excel at finding musical answers, but they need demonstrations from adults on the right process to use for any particular type of difficulty. Asking Guiding Questions ("What do you think of that F#?") instead of giving suggestions ("I think you should try to lower the F#") will narrow your child's focus and prompt them to fix the first thing that comes to their mind. As an added bonus, it's okay if you don't know the musical or technical answer to your question—all you have to do is ask!

## Procedures

Harnessing procedures in practicing is crucial because it removes the personal. "We always accomplish new techniques by chipping away at them together" is far more palatable to your child than, "Do that again!" Show that productive work on the instrument always involves a procedure—most often, this procedure includes analysis-based repetition. Many parents find that Guiding Questions is the easiest practice procedure to implement.

For example, a procedure for an advanced elementary-age student might be asking, "What do you think of the (tone quality, intonation) on that A-natural in measure seventeen?" In this instance, the Guiding Question is the procedure—it lets the parent control the productivity level of the practice session and helps child analyze their own playing. On the other hand, a procedure for a younger child might mean clapping a few notes, singing those notes, and then finally playing them on the instrument.

Emphasizing procedures that are based on constructive and reflective (technical and musical) criticism keeps productivity and motivational momentum strong. When musicians try to generate progress merely through mindless repetition (without analytical reflection like, "Was that note too high? Let me try it again and aim to be lower in pitch."), the results are usually unproductive. When things go right, young musicians are happy, but when things go wrong, players become agitated. They feel that something is wrong, but also find that they are not able fix it at will—how frustrating!

Work with your child's teacher to develop problem-solving procedures to make the most of practice time.

---

### Suspense

Parents and young musicians can bond over the suspense in the repetitions required to achieve new musical heights. This balance (of gritty persistence and patience for targeted, mindful repetitions) mirrors sports and our admiration for the perseverance and self-determination of high-achieving athletes. In hanging on each musical attempt like the next one could be the goal—SCORE!—or one step closer—ALMOST THERE!—you enjoy persevering together.

---

## Agree on a Secret Code

One of my students, Rose, became frustrated listening to her mother, Kaydence, repeatedly correct Rose's bow hold. However, both Kaydence and Rose agreed a proper bow hold was essential, would take some time to develop, and that they were in it to win it. Together, they pioneered a plan: every time Rose needed to check her pinky, her thumb, or her instrument posture, Kaydence would just say, "blue," Rose's favorite color. Whenever Kaydence said, "blue," Rose would fix all of the above.

This approach accomplished two things: it took the agony out of having to listen to the list of items to check (The bow! The thumb! The pinky!) by grouping them all together in one term, and it toned down the potential for frustration by using a totally neutral word. To this day, Rose receives compliments from other violinists in the studio about her excellent bow hold, posture, and technique.

### Take the Easy Way Out

One secret to effective criticism is to limit the number of words you need to say out loud. You can supercharge your communication style by finding clever ways to replace conversations. If it's easier to place a mat with drawn-on footprints on the floor than it is to argue with your child over how they should stand when they practice, do so. Replacing words with physical cues makes following instructions more palatable to your child.

For example, instead of repeating phrases like, "Fix your bow hold," simply hold up a sign that says, "bow hold." Teacher supply stores have little cardstock animal cutouts that are ideal for these cues.

Through strategies like this, you and your child will bond over your special secret language, and you won't even have to say a word out loud. Taking the easy way out means picking your battles wisely. Save your mental resources and patience whenever you can.

## Celebrate

As adults, we can get so hooked on a task and the thrill of completing it that we forget to acknowledge the small steps along the way. Children, however, need to understand the significance of each small step. Recognizing small victories—a fixed note here, more thorough vibrato there—teaches children how to value the learning process. Additionally, drawing attention to successful improvement helps children retain the techniques and nuances they do well. Because of this, well-timed praise partners well with criticism. You don't have to give out the musical equivalent of a participation trophy for every note, but you do need to consistently examine the balance between praise and effort as your child matures.

To make achievement recognition more meaningful, say your child's name during happy practice moments. Names are a shortcut to emotional identity for all of us, but many parents address their child by name primarily when the child demonstrates undesirable behavior. Instead, use your child's name when they have done something well. Comments like, "Wow, Jake, I LOVE to see you work on those double-stops!" are hugely motivational: they express both joy and pride. What an effortless way to create extra happiness during practice!

## Acknowledge Attention Spans

As a motivated adult, you can focus on a project for just about as long as you want to, provided the task is worth the effort to you. For children, their attempts on any task—no matter how fun or important it is—will at some point become sloppy or frustrating if they have exceeded their current attention span limits. When young musicians start lessons, their attention span is much shorter than it will be a few months down the road, when they will have built up a tolerance for sustained effort and learned how to find joy in practicing persistent focus. However, especially early on in their musical educations, most players have a considerably shorter window for productive focus than their parents have.

When parents and teachers consistently work out a child's focus muscles, the child's attention span and tolerance for criticism grow. By contrast, demanding an advanced focus level from the beginning of musical study will often break focus muscles and cause the child to act out.

Recognize that your attention span—and the resulting level of effectiveness for you—differs from your child's. For example, you might feel in a practice session that your child is really onto something: "If we could just keep practicing for five more minutes, we could finish this whole page!" In these instances, it's tempting to just push through the last bit of effort with your child to reach whatever milestone is in sight. However, by letting your child set down their instrument when they show signs of fatigue, you preserve their good will for practicing with you. Rather than limiting productivity, these recharge breaks extend the amount of content you can cover with your child each day.

## Read Body Language

Successful communication hinges on seeing where any conversation is going. Take note of your child's body language to anticipate their changing emotional state as a practice session wears on—this will be your first clue that you might need to change practice tasks or take a break in order to extend your child's positive mood.

For example, middle and high school musicians may hit their heels together (side steps) when they feel frustrated or flustered. Elementary and middle school musicians lean away from their instruments, rocking slightly and shifting their weight to the back of their feet. When a child's eyes wander to the door, ceiling, or clock, they're tuning out and waiting for the practice session to end. To bring focus back to the task at hand, direct your young musician to spy on their fingers or bow. Interestingly, this recharged focus actually makes the time pass much more quickly.

For young children, a break can be as small as doing a few jumping jacks or as big as taking the dog for a walk. Either way, cueing in to body language will keep you within the boundaries of effective communication. This awareness will extend the amount of work you can do with your child each day without frustration.

Many little children won't admit during a lesson or practice session that they need to go to the bathroom. Be proactive and accomplish this task before it's time to work together. Young children are unable to focus, remain still, or behave well when they are physically uncomfortable.

## Evaluating Productive Emotions

Assess whether emotion is playing a purely positive or frequently negative role in practice sessions. Look for cues for negative and positive emotions—what technical or musical difficulties cause a particular practice session to be exciting or frustrating? Are the levels of positivity in practice sessions based on how much energy you and your child have together on that particular day?

Ask your child and even yourself, "Which feelings help us here and which ones hurt us? What actions on my part and yours cause these feelings?" Determine the key words that bring you closer as well as the words or actions that only add to negativity or frustration during practice. By acknowledging the power of your child's emotions during practice and cueing into events before your child gets upset, you can steer practicing in the right direction.

Similarly, use humor to rest your child's focus for a few minutes during practice sessions. Find books of musical jokes, break out some board games, and try silly challenges like practicing in every chair in the house to keep practice sessions engaging.

While it may seem like this fun merely offers a distraction from practice session goals (or might prevent you from making efficient use of practice time), many children need the mental resets this laughter provides to avoid feeling overwhelmed or frustrated. Silliness breaks up repetitions and makes each one seem like a challenge (all part of the game!) instead of a mandate.

Let your child win these practice games. Remember, the true effort should be in the notes, not in the side game. The families in my own studio swear by Candy Land for its light-hearted nature and quick game time. Monopoly, Risk, and Sorry! are too involved for effective use in practice sessions.

Consider too how humor might be helpful or harmful. While it's wonderful to laugh with your child at funny notes, be careful to not let them perceive that you are laughing at their playing. A child will quit if they even suspect that their serious attempts are laughable. Here's the simplest formula: if your child laughs at something, smile and laugh. If they are serious, don't. It's one thing to find amusement in silly notes together, but it's important to avoid even unintentionally giving the impression that your child's work or best efforts seem foolish.

## Troubleshooting

Understand that you could be the perfect parent, with the perfect child, and all things in the universe could be wonderful, and yet, at some points you and your child might experience frustrating or tearful practice moments. The only way to avoid these difficulties is to be alone and pursue nothing. If you give up when confronted with these frustrating moments, you unintentionally demonstrate a lack of persistence to your child. They may perceive it as a lack of confidence (on your part) in their future and their ability to work through difficulties.

Use tough moments to model resilience, grit, and positive perseverance. Helping your child to develop these soft skills represents the ultimate benefit of musical and educational pursuits.

## The Price of Perfectionism

Perfectionism is always the elephant in the room in discussions about young artists. A frequent parental hope is that someday soon no one will be able to notice any performance mistakes from their child. Along with this sometimes comes a secret joy in hearing the mistakes other performers make. Young performers and their parents are eager to reach the playing level of those "big kids who *never* mess up."

However, experienced parents of young musicians understand that as their child grows and develops on the instrument, everyone's ears begin to improve. Mistakes in an older, advanced player that might have gone unnoticed as your family pushed through the "Twinkle phase" are now obvious as your child performs the Mendelssohn Violin Concerto. Teachers, parents, and players alike will be happiest when they recognize it is their ears' job to push instrumental performance to the next level by hearing and analyzing mistakes and finding room for advancing their technique. Therefore, perfection is a terrible goal in and of itself—the only way to truly achieve it would be to limit our ears' incredible ability to facilitate improvement.

Setting a goal like achieving the "perfect" performance of a piece would imply that all of the work—and, therefore, of the growth—should be completely over at the end of the performance. Why would anyone wish this on a child? Instead, take satisfaction in this neverending growth process and the huge source of motivation it can be!

So why is it that society views perfectionism as an admirable trait? For starters, it's much easier to ask for perfection than it is to provide specific routes to improvement. During lessons, teachers routinely hear phrases like, "Sweetie, make it perfect! Attention to detail! Fix those little things!" from parents to children. When a parent feels out of touch with the exact lesson content, admonishing a lack of detail or expressing a desire for perfection seems to cover all bases. This is counterproductive because these requests for perfection replace the nuanced constructive criticism that would actually facilitate improvement.

This desire for perfection is tricky to leave behind because it never comes from a cruel or mean place. Parents, do you ever believe that you (as a member of society) might feel more loved or secure if you had a more highly developed skill or talent to offer (performances as a prima ballerina, more spoken languages, widespread recognition in your career field)? We all feel that way to some extent, and many of us look back on our own childhoods with some regret for the talent we never fully developed. So, we start all over again on the next generation, determined to not let our children repeat our mistakes.

**In our eagerness to give young musicians the chance to develop the talent we never attained, we crush their creative impulses by offering our best advice in the form of perfectionism instead of through specific steps to improvement.**

One of my own teachers, violist and London Telefilmonic founder Levine Andrade, found a way to praise progress without lowering standards or expectations. As I tried to capture the right technique in the Walton Viola Concerto, he would call out, "That's very nearly very very good!" At first, I was baffled—was my playing good? Almost good? Almost very very good? Then I realized that Levine meant that I was on to something with my work, and while it wasn't ready yet, he could already see potential. Together, we weren't going to settle for just *good*, and we weren't going to blame any repetitions for their lack of perfection, either. We were going to keep working, because at the end of the day, things would be *very very good.*

Levine embraces this particular stage of learning and understands its meaning. He knows that you can recognize the quality of a piece that's still in the working stages and he teaches players how to believe in a project right from the start. This is a defining characteristic of effective teachers.

Consider this: you don't fault a cake for needing twenty-five minutes to bake in the oven—even the best ingredients require assembly and time. The same is true for young musicians. Trial and error (through deliberate practicing and lessons) is the assembly, and muscle memory (developed over the course of days or weeks) is the time. We can't skip the "baking" phase of any learning procedure.

Perfectionism is debilitating because it ignores these crucial learning stages. By contrast, declaring from the bottom of one's heart that the best is there to capture (through persistence) is empowering. Teach your child to have the strong conviction that their efforts will be rewarded and that they have an innate spark of competence. Don't just tell them they have talent. Talent is too flimsy: it has a reputation for being doled out randomly by fate or luck. Why leave something so big as hope and faith in one's own abilities to one's perception of the fates?! Instead, emphasize to your child that we are all born with that spark of competence. This spark does not prevent struggle. It does not entitle us to any ease or guarantee perfection. Instead, it allows for the defeat of inevitable difficulties.

Because musicians' ears will always be more advanced than their playing ability, no one—no matter how brilliant or noble!!—will ever achieve their goal if that goal is simply perfection. The greatest musicians in the world still hear areas for improvement, even if those nuances go beyond what most audiences can perceive. This trait, of always being able to hear one level more advanced than one can play, is what develops musical proficiency! Here's the catch: when young musicians expect to achieve total perfection and instead continue to hear areas for improvement, the experience might teach them that their efforts will never pay off as planned. As a parent, you can imagine how destructive this perception can be; it leads directly to learned helplessness.

To defeat the debilitating effects of perfectionism, teach your child to embrace the optimism, hope, and perpetual motivation that comes from simply believing that when one keeps working, improvement happens. Decide that you don't require perfection to be satisfied, modeling instead the notion that skills can always be improved through continuous effort. This approach facilitates both excellence and happiness in young musicians.

## Meliora

My own alma mater, the University of Rochester's Eastman School of Music, embraced this endless strive for improvement in our school's motto, *Meliora*, which means "Ever Better." *Meliora* captures the healthiest and happiest path to motivation, talent, and excellence for students of all ages and disciplines. *Meliora* demands no prerequisites—no matter where one starts, striving for self-betterment leads to excellence. No matter how the beginnings of a journey first appear, *Meliora* is there to help.

You can have full confidence in your child's musical potential, even when they are the three-year-old with the squeaky violin. Do this by understanding that every day, no matter what, your child's musical journey helps you both become ever better. Obstacles and mistakes provide opportunities to further creativity, critical thinking, and perseverance. Insisting on perfection merely gives voice to a young musician's insecurities and increases confusion, so instead embrace *Meliora*. Ask your child's teacher how to constructively find paths forward from any musical challenge.

---

### Transitioning to Solo Practice

Understandably, parents are eager for children to be able to practice productively without supervision. Bearing this goal in mind, recognize that (especially in the beginning) it is your job as the parent to model each aspect of the practicing process daily. This transition from supervised to unsupervised practice follows a different timeline for every young musician, but effective teachers will coach parents on how to handle it.

---

## Five Counterproductive Parent Habits & Phrases

Many parents are aware of the gap between their intentions and the actual effect specific parental actions have on children—sometimes, things just backfire. Even the smallest gestures can have stunningly negative effects. Over time, these unintentional and seemingly insignificant communication habits, though unnoticed by parents and unremarked upon by children, negatively impact the way children approach performance, practicing, and academics. Here are the most common communication mistakes teachers witness in lessons. The typical reaction from children is that they become quiet or start to play half-heartedly.

## Gasps, Sighs, and Eye-Rolls

When parents exhibit these gestures in reaction to any note, their child's heart sinks. Why would a child want to play when they perceive parents expressing disappointment or revulsion at the sound of their instrument? At moments in this learning process, parents will inevitably feel frustrated or disappointed—that's okay! However, expressing these sentiments during practice sessions or lessons creates a negative atmosphere. These small gestures don't build up players or advance technique. Instead, they stir feelings of hopelessness and incompetence.

## Vague Criticism

"Something is wrong there. Something doesn't sound right." This is a common statement from parents when they feel they don't know enough about music to help their child solve a specific technique issue on the instrument. How frustrating for everyone involved! However, embracing Guiding Questions is a productive strategy in moments like this. Here are a few questions to get you and your child started: "What do you think is going on in this measure? Can you pinpoint the funny note for me? Can you teach me this part? Let's brainstorm about what's tricky here."

When working with your child, show your willingness to engage with even the smallest details—otherwise, they might perceive that the material is beyond their grasp, too. "If my dad gives up, why should I keep trying?" is inevitably how the voice of doubt and fatigue will work itself into their perspective.

## "No"

As much as everyone wants practice to sound beautiful, weird sounds happen. It almost always takes several attempts to improve something. Rather than telling your child NOT to do something ("Don't squeak on the E-string!"), find something to give them TO do instead. Giving your child an action to take is far more effective than telling them that a musical element is undesirable. For example, "Check your bow—is it still straight?" is more productive than, "Stop that squeak!"

Here's an example of how this approach played a role in my own development. My first violin teacher, Nina Westbrook, excelled— and still excels—at these positive verbal gymnastics. In our lessons together, she could fix any odd note without having to use the word *no*. My parents marveled at this. Surely, at some point, with three-year-old violinists, you simply *must* tell them *no*. Three-year-olds sometimes behave horribly! They cry, scream, wander around the room, and mistreat their instruments! Three-year-olds give any sane adult dozens of reasons to shout "NO!" daily. Nina's lessons, though, were filled with warmth—in experiencing her kindness each week, I wanted to demonstrate my best behavior and wanted to fix each little task in my playing, even as a small child.

Achieving the perfect "sans-no" practice session is truly challenging. Still, eliminating *no* and replacing it with a positive task greatly improves a child's relationship with parents, teachers, and music. Productivity and the positive emotional trends skyrocket.

Of course, there's a counterargument to this philosophy. It's easy for parents to imagine that if they do not tell their child *no* when necessary, their child will turn into a full-blown monster by elementary school. This is understandable: it just means that it's important for every parent to draw their own boundaries. Whenever possible, replacing *no* with appropriate commands or actions will draw out the best response and most positive growth from the child. Used only when truly necessary, *no* has more impact and meaning. To achieve this consistently at home, discuss with your partner and music teacher how you might balance substitute commands ("Show me your bow hold.") with *no* ("Don't wave around your bow!").

## Next-Room Criticism

"SOMETHING DOESN'T SOUND RIGHT. SLOW DOWN AND FIX THAT!" You may be busy around the house and just trying to be helpful to your child at the same time, but instructions given from another part of the house rarely result in meaningful aid. Additionally, when you shout from a nearby room that your child needs to correct a technique, you unintentionally imply that whatever work you're actually doing is more urgent or important than sitting down with your child and practicing. Even when this is true, and your attention is needed elsewhere, avoid giving your child this impression.

## This Again?!

"We talked about this already! I told you to fix your pinky! You know better!" No teacher, parent, or child wants to experience the same issues over and over. However, even with the highest level of focus from a student, many musical challenges demand considerable mindful repetitive effort, including the significant time it can take to reprogram muscle memory. To ignore the necessity of this difficult yet invaluable learning process is damaging in two ways.

First, it belittles the value of devoting focused and repeated attention to the problem being fixed. There is no way to progress by simply powering through practice mindlessly. Here, it's important for young musicians to learn that they have the ability to overcome difficulties with persistent effort.

Second, ignoring the magnitude of such challenges implies that the child is somehow less intelligent or less hardworking than desired. If it were easy or even possible to achieve new techniques or modify old techniques on the instrument the first time around, everyone would be able to play Paganini. How unfair and disheartening, then, for teachers and parents to imply that all difficulties on a musical instrument should be fixed forever upon first mention. Children may not be able to articulate this frustration, but they feel it. It's incredibly demotivating and discouraging.

Occasionally, when a child has tried and failed at first or second attempt to fix something, they will try to show you, the parent, that they physically can't accomplish the task. The child will then take the extraordinary measure of blaming some perceived physical defect ("See? My pinky doesn't move like that; it's FROZEN!") to put the responsibility on their body instead of on themselves. This is an especially common response from children ages three through ten. It goes without saying that you certainly do not want your young musician to purposefully put obstacles in their own path. Instead, show them your respect for persistence.

## Evaluating Criticism

Appropriate criticism supports your child's self-esteem, teaching them to push their current boundaries and continually strive for better results. Positive, caring critique demonstrates that you value effort and believe in their potential, even while recognizing the inevitable difficulties. Effective criticism takes into account your child's capacity to focus and to process meaningful critique, and stays within these bounds to maximize positive productivity and foster self-motivation.

# Chapter 4

# Two-Column Learning: Music as a Vessel for Higher Pursuits

WHAT DOES MUSIC teach besides the notes? What does music leave its students with, even if they grow up to pursue other professional paths? Every music student wants to develop proficiency on their instrument and admirable tone quality, both of which are inherently rewarding. But what young musicians learn about themselves in the process of developing talent bodes even more for their future careers, happiness, and relationships. Two-Column Learning describes the concept of using a particular subject—music—as a medium for teaching essential life skills.

Through the study of music, children sharpen and routinize self-discipline, persistence, creativity, and collaboration. Developmental psychologists call these *soft skills*. These traits are difficult to attain yet crucial to success.

In supporting your child's pursuit of mastering a musical instrument, you provide them with a platform to appreciate their own ability to learn: the study of music becomes a basis for developing life skills. This means that rather than fixating solely on conquering instrument-specific hard skills (vibrato, tone quality) to get the grade or prize, our real job as parents and educators is to identify and build the soft skills needed (persistence, active listening).

With appropriate soft skills, other feats become much more achievable. An example of this is found in studies of college graduates, who tend to do well in life not just because they took all the right technical classes for their degree, but because they continued to learn for longer, consistently developing essential soft skills to a later age.

Studying music is a rich source of valuable lessons because it creates more "problems" for children to solve than simpler studies do. Music's complexity drives academic growth, attention to detail, and self-direction. The little-known reality here is that the lifelong gift of being able to play music is really just the icing on the cake! As a parent, when you feel stuck by technique or content in a practice session with your child, ask yourself, "How can I help my child learn the more valuable (soft skills) lesson here?"

Here's how to apply Two-Column Learning to your child's daily musical studies. If you're the parent of a five-year-old "pre-Twinkle" cellist, your left column might contain the song "Twinkle, Twinkle, Little Star." Your right column would contain soft skills like persistence, detail, patience, and respect for the instrument. As the parent of an older violinist working on memorization, your left column might list your child's current concerto. Your right column would list strategy, structure, repetition, routine, and confidence.

Young musicians rarely experience success in Column I without first developing the soft skills in Column II. Focusing on only the musical skill column, without positive parental involvement in the complete Two-Column Learning process, typically leads to frustration. When Column I is seen as the end-all be-all, the real learning opportunities (in Column II) are missed.

**Two-Column Learning Examples**

| Musical Skill | Learning Skill |
| --- | --- |
| Playing "Twinkle, Twinkle, Little Star" | Persistence, detail, patience; Respect for the instrument and teacher |
| Vibrato | Ability to follow instructions; Daily practice |
| Productive Daily Practice | Problem-solving, discipline, self-direction; Ability to accept suggestions for improvement |
| Memorization of Solo Works | Strategy, repetition, confidence |

For example, when children learn algebra, they are taught to follow well-established rules and push through procedure-based work. A seeming lack of creativity in mathematics drill leads many to claim that the subject has little relevance to them, especially if they believe they won't ever need to use the Distributive Property as adults. Kids may use this as an excuse to feel lukewarm about math, but we can confidently assure them that studying the subject benefits them anyway: it teaches how problems can be solved through logical procedures. Truly, this is what students need to take away from mathematical studies, regardless of whether they pursue the subject as adults.

Especially in the age of Google, knowledge about specific facts tends not to be as valuable as the process for finding and evaluating those facts. Point out to your children that it's not about just knowing answers in the form of mathematical numbers or musical notes. The true gain is in the soft skill: the ability to generate solutions (musical, mathematical, or other).

## Hold Up Your End of the Bargain

Two-Column Learning is based on a simple contract: if you want your child to be spectacularly good at the musical achievements in Column I, you have to be spectacularly patient when building the soft skills in Column II. You must keep believing in your child when all common sense would lead to giving up and pursuing easier activities.

Some people believe that for a child to be talented, the parent must also be talented. For example, Wolfgang Amadeus Mozart's father (Leopold) was a musician, so the younger Mozart had a huge advantage pursuing music as a child. However, parental talent is not a requisite for the Two-Column Learning contract. Two-Column Learning is based on the principle that for a child to grow musically, parents only need to have unwavering persistence. The trick is in the sequence of events. Your end of the bargain comes first—before you hear so much as one folk song from your child, they will see a lot of patience and persistence from you.

## Focus on the Right Difficulties

Pursuing Two-Column Learning means understanding where your child is in their lifelong learning process. If your child is at the stage where the teacher must tell them fifty times to correct a specific element of their technique, that's where they are. It's tempting to distract them out of frustration and slip in additional comments during lesson. "AND STRAIGHTEN YOUR BOW, MIA!" seems like a thorough way to end their teacher's original comment about vibrato. However, their teacher has most likely already noticed the flaw you pointed out and, for the sake of helping your child focus on the learning obstacle that is most important at that very moment, has chosen not to mention it yet. If this is the part of the process where the teacher points out your child's pinky, don't distract your child by badgering them about how the pinky AND the thumb should have been fixed forever last week.

Teachers call this selective commenting "editing" their lessons. If a teacher mentions absolutely everything that's wrong or not yet ideal with every note their student plays, the student will never get through so much as one page per lesson. Trust your teacher's judgment—you hired them for a reason! They have helped students with problems identical to your child's. They most likely have found an ideal progression for resolving the difficulties.

Some teachers cite parental interruptions in lesson as a reason for asking students to attend lessons alone. To these teachers, it's easier to cut parents out of the picture than it is to train parents to avoid distracting students in class. Parents, you don't want a teacher who thinks it's easier to lose you (and the assistance you might give between lessons) than it is to train you.

Instead, observe the way your child's teacher edits each lesson. You can learn how to do this editing at home when you help your child practice, and you can teach them how to edit their own playing as they mature. When your child is able to edit effectively, they achieve truly self-directed practicing!

To model editing during home practice sessions, just identify the most important thing (and only that one thing!) for your child to learn or modify at that moment. Think of your practice session as resembling the spaces in the board game Candy Land, with each space representing a single positive action. It's your job as the supervising parent to choose just one landing space (one task) at a time when you practice with your child.

## Weaknesses as Strengths

Strengths are flexible and fluid, changing as we develop through our lives. For example, if we start out weak in one area, it's sometimes a sign that the right work will help us become the very best in it. Similarly, for purposes of developing strengths (focus and self-discipline, for example), being found wanting can be even more ideal for a child than starting out sufficiently adept. Children become especially proficient in abilities that they must persistently pursue. In this sense, everyone needs a little "pet monster" (stage fright, discipline, technique) to battle in the practice room. Truly, it is far better to work on these things when a child is young rather than when they (and the monsters) are older.

Consider it this way: which player will become more proficient in tennis—the one who gets slow balls hand tossed to them or the one who plays earnestly against the tennis ball machine? With this frame of mind, parents can embrace difficulties, understanding that challenges are absolutely essential to musical and personal growth.

By contrast, some parents accidentally sabotage their children's growth opportunities. For example, holding a child back one year or more in orchestra may allow that child to be older than their peers, but this does not necessarily contribute to better emotional or musical growth. The high ensemble chair that an age advantage might facilitate is not the most important reward for learning—developing a positive approach to challenging educational curveballs will bring the bigger long-term payoff.

Viewed this way, how debilitating it would be to never encounter sufficient challenges as a child! When parents filter a child's experiences to ensure success at every turn, the child receives the following messages: *Things should be easy, so I won't give you challenges I think you can't handle. If something is hard, it's not worth pursuing. I don't believe in you yet. You should only pursue something when you're confident you can be the best in it.*

To remedy this perspective, strive to provide suitable challenges and then provide support as needed. When you do this, you build your child's collection of pet monsters—the nerves of that very first concert, a fancy new piece assigned by the teacher, speaking in public for the first time. Start with small monsters and work your way up. Avoid confronting your child's monsters for them (for example, delaying the first recital until your child is the oldest participant or selecting a less competitive school over a highly ranked one). Instead, teach your child to take pride in battling challenges, even when (as with nerves) they start out scary.

## "We're in This Together"

Parents confess that they feel guilty when their child struggles with the same difficulties they themselves once faced. This guilt provokes in them two reactions.

In the first, they attempt to immunize their child. "I failed at violin, so I force my child to practice two hours every day." In response to this pressure, the child often rebels and refuses the instrument entirely.

The second parental reaction is fear about challenging their child with a difficulty that the parents themselves haven't fully overcome. "Ooh, scary, a recital! I never could play well at recitals!" they might say, half-teasingly. An even more common concern manifests as, "I never practiced when I was young, so I don't feel like I'm being fair when I demand more practicing from my child."

Two-Column Learning comes to the rescue in these situations. When your child struggles with something (from stage fright to scheduling regular practice sessions) you find intimidating, be open about the soft skill your child has the chance to build. When difficulties arise with getting kids to practice, parents can be open about these challenges without assigning blame ("Alex is never motivated to practice!"). I have heard parents use this characterization to feel less at fault themselves, in an attempt to feel less embarrassed in front of the other adult in the room (the teacher) when their child is simply unprepared for class.

Instead, it's far better to say, "We're working on that practice routine, but it's tougher than we thought." It is not a fault to take responsibility for things like a child having a cranky lesson because they aren't well-rested. This is all part of the normal learning process, and no one gets to skip over it. We can all try our best, but even the most disciplined families experience hiccups like this.

If you are concerned that your child seems less motivated than others, ask their teacher what is normal for students in your child's age group and playing level. Teachers can tell you what skills matter most through each phase of the musical development process.

Sometimes the best thing to do is acknowledge when your child has reached a struggle stage. "Yes, we fight over practice times. Yes, we're frustrated over developing focus." Acknowledging that everyone in the family is working together to overcome challenges makes it possible to take appropriate steps without anyone (especially your child) feeling attacked or guilty. Even a rough week or month represents a positive step forward in the journey to improve musically.

## Manage Expectations to Prompt Positive Behavior

Before you leave for a trip, you plan. You know how you will to get there, what you will eat, and what the weather will be like. You know to bring sunscreen to the beach or pack gloves for skiing. As adults, we often take for granted how much comfort our ability to plan for the immediate future brings. Because young children don't have this power, it's up to you to give them the same comfort by setting their lesson expectations clearly and repeatedly. In so doing, you give them the chance to put their best foot forward. Clear expectations lead to positive Column II soft skill behaviors, which of course determine the technical achievements in Column I.

The first way to set expectations is to ask questions. "Can you imagine what it will be like to play piano? I'm so excited for us to work on music together! Are we finally going to our first lesson today?" There's no such thing as asking too many fun questions or building up too much hope. The more thrilled and proud your child is to begin their musical journey, the easier it will be for them to work with their teacher.

The next way to set expectations is to talk with your child about what kind of behavior you would like to see during lessons. For children under five, you might even have them act out simple tasks like standing in one place or keeping their eyes on the teacher. It's okay to drill the scenarios and behaviors you would like to see as long as the repetition is positive. To further facilitate mental preparation, take a drive by the teacher's studio with your child before attending the first class.

You can help your child live up to everyone's expectations by ensuring they have slept well, snacked on some protein, and visited the restroom before the lesson starts. In establishing this pre-lesson routine, you demonstrate to your child how physical well-being affects their ability to learn effectively. Avoid rushing—it's easier to be grumpy to kids (without even realizing it!) when you are running late. Your mood can be contagious to your child right before they need to achieve peak focus.

Expectation management helps musicians learn how to appreciate advanced concerts and art at a young age. While attending a full symphony concert might be rough for those whose ages are in the single digits, setting appropriate behavior and etiquette expectations and leaving promptly when kids show signs of fatigue (at intermission or during applause) gives them a chance to grow musically without wearing out their good mood.

## Look for the Hidden Story

One evening in the early 2000s, my brother and I were frantically rehearsing for a performance. Our rehearsal together with our mother ended in all the usual protests—screams, tears, and threats of never playing music with each other ever again. The next evening, as we performed together, another mother walked by with her two children. My own mother overheard her. "SEE, there's a brother and sister playing together!" the mother admonished her children. My mother couldn't help but think that had that woman attended our family rehearsal the previous night, her appraisal of our dynamic duo might have been a little different.

Fortunately for my brother and me, our parents never actually reacted to our protests or allowed us to cancel a gig because of bickering. They understood that every performance has a backstory, and if we were at the stage where our backstory included calling each other names until 9 p.m., then so be it. We would be happy and professional in public the next day. In this case, our Column I duet performance happened because we had the Column II perseverance to play in public together even after a rough rehearsal.

## We All Visit Mess City

One of the most significant things the study of music teaches is that art from even the pickiest people starts out messy, inconvenient, and difficult. As an adult, the messy part to you might be the moment your child refuses to pick up their violin. For your child, the messy part might be when the instrument squeaks instead of sings. Embrace your messy difficulties to model for your child how they can embrace theirs. Ease is not a prerequisite for high art, but difficulty often is. Remind yourself and your child that whenever things seem most bleak, that's simply the part of the process you're in right now—you're in Mess City. You can't skip over it on the map of your child's musical journey; you've got to go right through it with them if you want to get to the other side. Put your family's musical goals in Column I, and when you and your child get to Mess City, put patience for those inevitable squeaky violin noises or frustrating practice sessions in everyone's Column II.

## Troubleshooting: Pre-K Musicians

*"Why are we spending $45 each lesson when Sarah just throws temper tantrums and cries the whole time! It's a waste of our money and her teacher's time! Is it worth it? Is Sarah really*

*learning anything? Can we just start again in a few years? I don't know why Sarah acts like this every time I come near her with the violin. Do other kids have this many problems?!"*

You start an exciting new activity with your child and, a few weeks in, things start looking rough. Your child is no longer in love with the lesson material and they ignore their teacher. They put obstacles in their own way and they seem to do it just to irk you. With all the resources your new pursuit takes, you consider whether it's worth it. You wonder whether your child has the maturity to even justify the effort and expense on your part.

Teachers tell parents that this is a common experience. The way you guide your child through moments like this will have a lasting impact on development. Success here is about more than growing up with a talent for violin, ballet, or soccer. Success means teaching your child how to understand where they are in the learning process and how to push through the inevitable (guaranteed!) difficulties. It's one thing to tell children to persevere through all, but it's another to demonstrate that approach day in and day out yourself.

Persevering through these difficulties is much easier said than done. Many parents at the start of their child's musical journey give up and resolve to try lessons again in a few years. All the expense, patience, and tears, just to play "Twinkle" at three rather than five— is it worth it? Absolutely. Starting younger fundamentally changes the way your child grows to interact with their instrument, and has huge implications for their future muscle and ear development. It's not that you spent $5,000 learning "Twinkle" that first year. You spent $5,000 on "Twinkle" *and* all of your Column II learning skills: behavior development, ear training, rhythmic listening, maturity.

Go for it! Overcoming these difficulties as a team is an investment in your relationship with your child.

So, your child has a tantrum in a lesson—don't ruminate about how the class is now a waste of tuition, even if the monetary cost stings. Remind yourself that this is the stage you and your child are going through now to gain skills in both Column I and Column II. It's not just about the notes, it's about learning to work effectively as a teacher-student-parent trio.

When your child throws a fit, they're watching for your reaction. How are you going to respond? What are you going to show them? If you quit or leave class, you show them that nothing is worth pursuing if it comes with a tantrum. Before doing so, consider what better message you might send instead. The right message is that you are willing to wait the tantrum out. Prove that tantrums don't rattle you or their teacher. No matter how wonderful any three-year-old is, tantrums happen. Before starting lessons, plan how you will react.

## The Link Between Productivity and Physical Comfort

Our first job as parents and teachers is to provide a safe learning environment. Our second job is to provide the actual musical and technical content. It is impossible for children to engage with musical learning when they feel uncomfortable or upset. Small children will feel cranky when they haven't slept well or they're distracted.

These issues are common, and parents can work to ensure that they are taken care of before lesson starts. However, sometimes toddlers come to their lessons in the middle of a bad day and the events leading up to the lesson simply can't be helped. In this circumstance, some parents desperate to ensure learning during lesson time resort to strict discipline that only upsets children further, thereby bringing the lesson's productivity to a complete halt.

As a teacher, I've been horrified to watch parents threaten to spank their children if the child (usually between age three and five) didn't calm down and behave for the duration of their lesson. With this young age group, temper tantrums are usually the result of a lack of sleep the night before, unclear expectations about behavior, frustration with the instrument, or insecurity over their own ability to play well in front of parents and teachers. This combination leads to acting out, which is understandably frustrating for parents. Threats of spanking, however, only add to a child's feelings of embarrassment and frustration.

After all, what child would ever want to touch the violin again if the instrument could even remotely be blamed for physical pain (spanking) from the person they love most in the world (their parent)? With little musicians, behavior is a problem not because any one child is willfully disruptive, but because small children in general are still learning how to focus with their parents and teachers for extended periods of time. And because age three doesn't equip everyone with a nuanced ability to communicate insecurities or discomfort, acting out is the solution most toddlers and pre-K students try first.

Through situations like this, we need to remind ourselves as teachers and parents that this is just where we are in our Two-Column Learning pursuit. Perhaps we are just at that stage where the child confronts soft skills as simple—yet crucial!—as following instructions from their teacher, or staying happy in lessons. Resorting to any type of physical discipline to remedy behavior issues will never bring us closer to our children or to musical achievement. Understanding that emotional growth is an essential part of musical growth will help us keep calm through any storm that even the youngest violinist throws. By viewing these tantrums as a mere bump in the road, instead of a complete derailment, we remain on the path to musical excellence.

On a related subject, a dear friend of mine, a performer whose international competition wins sparkle on her résumé, has a scar on her hand (twenty-some years later!) from where her childhood piano teacher smacked her with a ruler. My friend has excelled musically despite this abuse, which should never be tolerated from teachers at any level.

Given that modern studies show the negative effect fear has on the brain's ability to learn, parents and teachers must strive to provide a safe and comfortable environment for musical growth. There will *never* be a situation in which physical discipline will be a positive and effective motivator for musicians of any age. Leave this method of discipline in the distant past, where it belongs.

# Part 2
# Establish Advanced Technique

# Chapter 5

# The Recipe for Positive Practicing

*"When we sit down to practice together, it always ends in a fight. She doesn't understand that I'm just trying to help her—she takes everything so personally!"*

*"He knows he has to slow down to fix intonation, but he still just plays through everything at 90 miles an hour. It gets so sloppy that by the time lesson rolls around, no one can tell that he even touched the violin at all."*

*"We had a few good days and then we left for vacation—by the time we got back, we were all a little rusty."*

## Initiating Musical Momentum

A violinist in motion tends to stay in motion. By contrast, a violinist watching *Friends* reruns (instead of practicing) tends to continue watching *Friends* reruns. Musically speaking, momentum is either with a child or it's against them. When a child is used to working for an hour on the violin each day, the time goes by quickly and they learn to self-direct progress. On the other hand, when it's been a few days since the last practice session, resuming work is much more tedious and intimidating. Truthfully, it's easier to maintain momentum (by practicing in short sessions daily) than it is to practice in bigger "emergency" sessions each time a school chair test or audition comes around. By the time deadlines like this approach, most players will have forgotten huge parts of their lesson material—this not only makes their work on their instrument more difficult, but also makes the time they spend practicing tick by more slowly. With experiences like that, no wonder some children dread practicing!

The most effective way to put musical momentum to work for your child in your family's practice routine is to grab a calendar and a set of stickers. Put a sticker on the calendar for every day the instrument comes out of the case (whether for a true practice session or just because your child doesn't want to lose the day's sticker).

Do follow through and give a sticker for absolutely every day the instrument comes out of the case, regardless of how many notes were played or how much time was spent practicing. Make it nearly impossible for your child to fail the first few weeks you build up this practice momentum. If there's one moment to toughen up and insist that something get done, this is it. Before your child can take advantage of the progress that consistent practice sessions bring, they must first get in the groove. Establishing musical momentum achieves that. As an adult, you have probably experienced how much easier it is to keep working on a current project than it is to switch to an activity you've long been neglecting. Likewise, let momentum work its magic for you and your young musician!

## Muscle Memory

Here's how muscle memory works: when you run daily, running becomes easier. Your legs become tuned with your mission and can be counted upon to propel you forward. Similarly, the physicality of playing an instrument means that violinists, for example, find it easier to play advanced works if they practice daily. They find it more difficult to play these same works when they have taken time off between practice sessions. In dealing with gaps like this, even when a musician remembers the score clearly and understands all of the presented techniques, they find that their fingers are just not able to be fast or accurate enough.

Professionals call this phenomenon muscle memory. It's the idea that musicians' hands aid in accuracy and speed when they are kept in shape by daily practice. A famous musical phrase is, "If I don't practice one day I know it. Two days, the critics know it. Three days, everyone knows it." This quote is attributed to everyone from Isaac Stern to Jascha Heifetz, proving that if we can all agree about one thing, it's the importance of daily finger work.

Frustration is the fastest way to deter a beginning musician from regular, voluntary practice, and maintaining muscle memory is the best way to avoid needless struggle. Who would want to practice if it seemed like they were endlessly repeating history, rebuilding the same muscle memory they had already established and then lost? Of course, there will be instances that make it difficult to practice consistently—vacations, major holidays, business trips. Still, it's well worth the effort to practice every possible day outside of these conflicts.

After any break, always emphasize a prompt return to the instrument to minimize the loss of muscle memory. For example, having your child warm up on their instrument a few minutes before departing for the airport on the first travel day will make a tremendous difference when they return to their practice routine—the extra session represents one fewer missed day. What a great chance for you and your family to demonstrate the impact of every single practice session!

## Follow the Recipe Exactly

As people, we excel at finding the most efficient way to accomplish a task—we tend to look for shortcuts even when given specific instructions. While efficiency can be an asset, occasionally it backfires. When young musicians and their parents expect to achieve a certain musical result on the instrument between lessons and fail, the fault is most often found in how loosely the week's practicing instructions were followed.

To illustrate this tendency, let me tell you a story. I have a dear friend, Ann Burckhardt, who has authored several cookbooks and wrote a regular newspaper column including her favorite recipes. After each week's column, she would inevitably receive calls from readers who were upset about the recipe—it didn't taste good, it took twice as long to bake, it was nothing like the picture. To make things worse, these cooking fiascos had often happened during a special family occasion, resulting in embarrassment. Callers were usually quite upset when they telephoned Ann.

Ann was always understanding and sweet to her readers to help them learn where things had gone wrong. "Tell me, dear, did you follow the recipe exactly?" she would ask. Typically, the answer was something like, "Well, I didn't have chicken, so I used shrimp instead." Or, "I didn't have enough time, so I baked it at a higher temperature." Then, of course, came "I couldn't find any baking powder, so I just used baking soda and put in a little extra."

About two substitutions into the conversation, Ann would gently point out where the effort had, perhaps, gone wrong. When she calmly explained why baking powder was required instead of baking soda, her readers began to understand why their substitutions, not Ann's original and well-tested recipe, had caused the problem.

Here's why this is relevant to effective practicing: in an effort to accommodate whatever else is going on, it's easy to overlook just how damaging substitutions and shortcuts are to a young musician's development. For example, we may know we are supposed to work for thirty minutes per day according to a teacher's instructions, but because Saturday slipped away we find ourselves fifty-two minutes into Sunday's now hour-long practice session with our young musician in tears of frustration over something that should have been accomplished yesterday.

In other moments, we find ourselves cutting corners by shouting instructions from the kitchen, or sneaking glances at the phone when we know we should be giving our full attention throughout each practice session. When assembling furniture, have you ever, in haste, disregarded the instructions only to have it turn out crooked, unstable, or flawed in some other way that IKEA should surely have thought to resolve?

It may feel silly and inconvenient to go all the way to the store to buy the baking powder, to let the cake bake for the full twenty-five minutes instead of just setting the oven at a higher temperature for twenty minutes, to read the assembly instructions cover to cover, and to fully power down all electronic devices whenever the violin comes out of the case. However, if you want an award-winning cake, you have to follow the award-winning recipe exactly. The minute you shortchange an ingredient, you are no longer following the award-winning recipe. In the end, it's well worth every extra effort to follow the practicing recipe (as given by your child's teacher) exactly.

**Achieving Consistent Practice Standards**

Is your child supposed to practice standing up or sitting down? Is it okay to have the radio or TV on in the background? Is your child allowed to dictate their own list of practice tasks, or do they need to work with you on a specific assignment from their lesson? Does time matter, or is practicing over when repertoire is memorized? By understanding the ground rules (ask your child's teacher for suggestions here), you enhance the productivity of every practice session.

## Missed Expectations

Despite good intentions, things don't always work out according to plan. Find success by making constructive examples of small failures (inevitable in any pursuit) to help children understand the nuanced relationship between goals, work, and results. Of course, the world is not always fair, and sometimes good work goes unrewarded because of outside factors. Most often, though, missed goals happen when young musicians fail to consistently put in the time and effort required to meet the expectations set by parents and teachers. The natural consequences that ensue are an important learning opportunity. Letting these consequences play out, even if painful at the time, is a highly effective way to teach that there is no compensating down the road for the progress missed today.

## Drill vs. Intentional Playing

*"But if I tell Anita to play it ten times in a row, she should just do that, right? That's not too much to expect from an eight-year-old,*

*and I feel like if she would just listen to me, we would finally be on the right path!"*

When Anita first started studying with me, her father, Joseph, was convinced that repetition during practice mattered more than anything else. He had a great point: repetition is a crucial part of musical proficiency. However, Joseph hadn't factored in that Anita, still in her first few months of violin study, was not yet able to make deliberate, nuanced improvements from one repetition to another. Anita merely played through her assigned folk songs, hoping notes would improve each time. When they did, she was happy to continue practicing, but when she missed notes, she became discouraged and frustrated.

The problem with drill (mindless repetition) during musical practice is that it leaves out the critical thinking required to consciously improve results. Before children understand the process of mindful repetition (deliberately tweaking elements of their playing to achieve better results), each new repetition creates unpredictable results. A child may be trying their best, but without an understanding of how technique fundamentals affect their sound, improvements are random at best. It takes time (and hard-earned maturity) for a young musician to learn to control their sound and self-direct practice effectively. This essential process cannot be replaced by or accelerated with mindless repetition.

When a young student finds that they can't fully control the sound results, they quickly grow frustrated. This presents an opportunity for parents and teachers to intervene to ensure efficient progress and spur motivation.

I explained to Joseph that Anita didn't yet know how to practice mindfully. Anita couldn't fully understand trial and error, and she couldn't generate (without prompt) the technical changes (a lower or higher bow arm, landing several fingers on the A-string simultaneously) that determine tone quality. All Anita knew is that sometimes when she played she and her father liked the sound, and sometimes they both hated it. Each time Joseph winced at a squeak, Anita gathered that trial and error wasn't an acceptable approach.

Joseph and I came up with a plan. First, he realized he truly needed to be involved in Anita's practice sessions—musical repetition without parental feedback at age eight is simply not productive. Second, he realized that in each practice session, he needed to display appropriate reactions to every earnest attempt.

Soon, Joseph began to model intentional playing, narrating with his own (full-sized) violin the arm movements he wanted to see from Anita. He even asked Anita to correct his own posture and bow hold. These strategies worked: Anita started to take more control of her playing when they worked together, and this self-direction carried over into the short bursts of practicing she did alone. She started modifying out-of-tune notes herself and began memorizing folk songs and scales before Joseph had even learned them.

By demonstrating his own intentional practicing, Joseph helped Anita realize the impact she could have on her own violin playing. Recently, Joseph mentioned to me that he overheard Anita (now nine years old) practicing in the next room as he arrived home from work and he found himself in tears at how spectacularly self-sufficient she was getting. He still complains occasionally, "When will Anita be able to do meaningful and mindful repetition totally without me?" but he sees the tremendous difference his behavior changes have made.

---

### Evaluate Your Own Focus

Rough practice sessions happen when we think we're focused on the child, but we are actually still carrying emotions or thoughts from something that happened earlier in the day. We may feel like we're hiding our lack of focus, but children still sense it. When we fail to fully engage them with eye-contact, responsive gestures, and nuanced communication, they begin to tune out.

If you find your work is preventing you from being fully focused on your child during practice, understand this is normal. It just means you need to consider whether your thoughts during practice are merely distracting or actually necessary. If you can't fix the work crisis while working with your child on violin, let this be your chance to push it out of your mind. Let the practice session recharge you: you will return to your source of stress fresh and ready to move forward.

---

## Understanding Task Size

Who doesn't love finishing an entire page of work? Reaching such a discrete and measurable milestone is inherently satisfying. However, merely playing through an entire assigned etude won't help musicians improve as much as focused, detailed work on the etude's trickiest passages will. Parents can spur progress here by teaching their children to transition from being page oriented (defining a page run-through as success) to being quality oriented.

For example, when one family in my studio started giving their son, Jamie, positive feedback based on individual practice tasks (instead of just awarding stickers for achieving a certain number of run-throughs), Jamie learned the power of mindful work and critical thinking. Not only did Jamie develop a more nuanced approach to learning each technical aspect of the piece, but he understood that when he quickly ran through his music, he neglected to create real change and therefore wouldn't progress as planned.

Discuss with your teacher what an effective practice session task size should be for your child. For example, is it best to isolate just one measure, one line, or half of a page? This will help you and your child identify your mission at any given moment of your practice session together. As a bonus, this targeted approach allows an appropriate pace of achievement, giving children a sense of satisfaction in their work.

## What *Work* Really Means

What does it mean to *work* on something? Does work start the moment the pencil touches the page or the bow glides over the strings? What about the preparation that has to happen before that?

Perhaps the definition of work is flawed. The perceived definition ("work: the exact assignment") undervalues related efforts. For example, perhaps the first step to working on your child's etude is helping them set up a practice timeline. Maybe working toward your family's musical goals means simply continuing with lessons, even though it's been some time since your child willingly practiced. Working on the cello sometimes means talking with your child about the value of sticking with an effort, though momentarily they might prefer to give up. All of these small steps are part of the larger picture of pursuing musical success while working on learning skills.

Understand that even the most fun work is still *work*. This is true no matter how much you or your child love a subject. If your child expects that all aspects of musical study should always be play and that something is wrong when the required efforts feel like hard work, they won't be happy in their musical pursuits. They might prefer to drop music in favor of truly mindless "play" activities.

Here's the remedy for this: avoid creating the expectation that playing an instrument will always be fun or effortless. By giving your child something to struggle with, you give them opportunities to learn that excellent results come through effort. Through consistent experiences like this, children develop the ability to direct positive improvement during practice. When they push through the occasional frustration or inconvenience, they move forward!

## Harness Boredom to Teach Self-Motivation

*"But, Mommmmm, I'm SO BORED. I HATE PRACTIC-ING. These etudes are SO BORING. Time has stopped, OKAY? TIME HAS TOTALLY STOPPED!!"*

What can be gained from studies that seem genuinely boring? Boredom is inevitable—for example, no matter how much a student loves math, there may eventually be a unit that seems irrelevant. Professional musicians emphasize that it's important to polish "boring" pieces to the same standard as "fun" ones.

When we allow children to step away from subjects they find dull ("We tried to introduce him to music, but he just wasn't interested—he didn't have the patience for it."), we unintentionally convey that all activities must be inherently interesting to be worthy of pursuit.

By contrast, if we force children to study something they don't like, the situation predisposes them to "I hate math!" sentiments. When a subject is so detested, every assignment is a burden on the entire family. Worse, when children don't fully engage with the required material, they lose the chance to master what could stepping stones for future studies.

Given that a natural interest in any subject makes memorization easier, developing your child's musical interest is key. Conveniently, the rich diversity of available musical genres offers children many avenues to pursue. For example, if classical pieces aren't your child's cup of tea yet, how about supplementing their studies with a little country fiddle music? Find a path to developing interest wherever possible, even if it means adding a little work by diversifying lesson content.

What does boredom in practicing mean? What causes it, and how can we take control of it? Let's start with the assumption that most fun work is inevitably going to entail some uninteresting tasks, no matter how much you love the subject. Powering through boredom routinely gives children the means to motivate themselves when boredom strikes again on future tasks.

The first way to introduce your child to boredom-defeating techniques is to teach them to set mini-goals during dull tasks. For example: "How many math drill pages can we do today?" "How neat can you make your letters?" "Isn't it fun to make a game of this assignment? I bet we can make a game with our other homework too!" "Can you think of a game you could play against yourself or the clock here?"

Teach your child to set goals on their own focus, especially when confronted with boring work. When the Boredom Monster begins to work for (rather than against) your child and their academic future, good things happen. Given that boredom causes fatigue to come on fast, it's in everyone's best interest to develop a game strategy for dull assignments!

## Understanding The Wall

Have you ever started a work assignment only to have your mind go completely blank? Fraught with writers' block, you dashed to the fridge, procrastinating with a snack. Or, alternatively, the little voice of hope in the back of your mind told you, "It's okay, this isn't due until Friday, check your email first and take care of this problem later."

If so, you have definitely experienced The Wall. The Wall is the feeling of overwhelm that causes you to procrastinate your work with mindless tasks. If you stare at your work without making a single step forward, you have still hit The Wall, you just haven't found a convenient distraction or excuse for procrastinating your work. Similarly, when students hit The Wall in lessons, their eyes glaze over and they lose their focus. As they realize how difficult a passage in their new concerto is, they start asking totally unrelated musical questions, stalling before they have to get to work on the intimidating technique.

On days you feel too tired to practice with your child, you too have hit The Wall. The first trick to pushing through it is just realizing that it's there. That's not so easy in the moment. Then, understand that The Wall is just there to scare you. Better yet, decide this particular challenge is just the sort of obstacle that might stop other parent-child teams but won't stop you.

The next secret to pushing through The Wall is noticing when, exactly, it tends to pop up in your weekly practice routine. Do you and your child both hit The Wall at about 8 p.m. on Thursday nights? Is it nearly impossible to practice productively after a soccer match? Do your best to avoid these triggers. For example, plan to cover the most difficult musical material at the beginning of practice sessions and avoid creating situations where practice is necessary late on a Thursday night or after your child's big game.

While avoiding triggers for The Wall helps productivity, regularly acknowledge to your child that these feelings—being overwhelmed, helpless, intimidated, or simply too tired—are common. When children practice and study as they should, they will use up their mental and physical resources on most days. Well-timed breaks keep The Wall at bay for as long as possible, but it will eventually interfere when there is still work to be done. When you and your child start pounding on The Wall, determined to break through, both of you will find new strength in your determination.

By discussing The Wall with young musicians, we teach them how capable they truly are, even when they feel like giving up. In doing so, we prepare them to confront future challenges. We give them the tools they need to find hope and progress when it might be easier to simply put off their work for another time.

## Consequences for Skipping Practice

When I was young, my father decided it would never be worth the family strife to shout at my brother or me if he wanted us to practice and we refused. Instead, he would just say, "Okay then, natural consequences," and leave it at that. At first, we would gleefully wander off to watch TV or do whatever else we wanted to do instead of practicing. Occasionally, my father would embellish his warning. "Okay then, natural consequences—you have thirteen days before the competition. That's not very long before natural consequences kick in." Usually, we would still choose our free-time activities over practice.

Soon, however, we would buckle down and practice, the threat of natural consequences from upcoming tests or competitions looming closer. My father would point out how stressed we were. "You see, guys? Natural consequences. If you don't like this frantic feeling, you need to remember it the next time you want to skip out on your practicing."

Inevitably, our poor choices caught up with us—we would have a terrible evening right before an audition, practicing like crazy in frustration (this was always unproductive and ineffective). When we were unprepared for lessons, our teachers called us out on it. The lesson about natural consequences stuck with us—embarrassment is a powerful motivator.

Our father never threw us under the bus in front of our teacher. He just let that week's playing speak for itself and reiterated at home, "Natural consequences, guys. You will always be able to skip out on work, but you will have to decide if it's worth the natural consequences to you."

My father knew what he was doing. He let us experiment with poor priorities and choices when we were young enough that our actions didn't yet carry life-altering consequences. It was just enough to cause us some regret or embarrassment—and usually enough that we wouldn't forget his advice. To this day, when I am tempted to procrastinate any kind of work, I ask myself if it's worth the natural consequences. My usual conclusion is that it's not.

## Tricks that Work for Any Instrument

### Play Games to Thwart Frustration

"We were so frustrated this week," one of my clients confessed in lesson as his daughter unpacked her violin. "Jenna just gets so *emotional.*" Jenna's father, Brian, wanted to help Jenna stay positive during practice sessions, even as it seemed her perfectionist tendencies would lead her to quit the violin if she couldn't learn to let them go.

The root of the problem was not bad at all—Jenna wanted to set high standards for herself (at age seven!) and play well for her father. In her eagerness to succeed, she didn't want to accept the necessity of giving particular techniques multiple tries. In Jenna's world, attempting a new note and getting a squeak from the violin more than once was surely a sign of her being, to use her own term, "bad." Even though Brian would assure Jenna that he wanted her to work with him through trial and error, Jenna was on a one-try-only mission. She didn't yet have the emotional patience to understand that effective practicing comprises of many attempts and improvements, not just a final product.

Explaining the benefits of trial and error to Jenna was not enough to convince her of the merit of working through measures or lines over and over—Jenna would still become upset and perceive that she was incompetent when she had to do this. We needed a way to diffuse the tension in the room between takes so Jenna could restart her mental count of how many tries she had "used up."

Jenna felt she was too old for "baby games." She didn't want to play Candy Land or do jumping jacks between repetitions. She did, however, find tic-tac-toe palatable. It was short and easy—she and her father simply kept a separate pad of paper on her music stand to keep score. It worked: tic-tac-toe was just enough of a game to give Jenna's patience a chance to reset between each musical attempt.

Like Brian and Jenna, you too can find creative ways to game your practice session with your child. This is especially important when the musical work you want to accomplish together might lead to frustration. When you make a practice task (for example, playing one measure for each move) part of a game, you bring positive excitement to the practice session—each repetition is an opportunity to create a new game victory. Children handle frustration better in game situations because the suspense (whether over conquering a musical difficulty or having the game-winning X in tic-tac-toe) makes the pursuit of practice tasks exciting in a positive, rewarding way.

## Practice Board (Feet)

When children struggle with the content (tricky notes) on the music stand, many take additional steps closer to the music itself. As people, we all fall for the powerful instinct of trying to get physically closer to whatever small thing we are trying to read or work on, especially when there is a particular note we don't yet understand. In practice sessions, this habit quickly leads to slouching, poor technique, and loss of tone quality. Similarly, when torsos and toes don't align with the upper body positioning, it's hard to create the angles necessary for proper bowing of stringed instruments.

For young or beginning musicians who are not yet as self-aware of their body positioning as advanced players, placing a practice board on the floor helps with both posture and focus. The classic educational tool makes it easy for players to keep their feet and their eyes right where they belong, thereby even minimizing the distractions that occur whenever family members walk by the room.

## Land Your Airplane

Many young musicians fall into the trap of trying to improve their playing while they run through pieces at full speed. This approach isn't effective. It's virtually impossible to create nuanced change with run-throughs. Here's how you can explain to your child the importance of stopping to work on small difficulties throughout their pieces: "Look, no matter how experienced a pilot is, they still have to land their airplane and put it in the garage before making repairs. Can significant repairs to an airplane be made while flying at full speed through the sky? Not really. The violin is just as complicated as an airplane—look at all these precise finger movements you do! Land your musical airplane—stop right at measure twenty-five, for example, and notice what you might like to fix. Play it slowly a few times, modifying each try, and then put that measure back into its musical context. Once you have worked on your 'repairs,' you can resume flying. Check these 'repair' spots daily to keep your playing in tip-top shape."

## Timer

Set timers to define the beginning and end of a practice session and to divide the session up into discrete task units. For example, one of my students, Michael, was exceptionally talented as a six-year-old. His musical level was far beyond his attention span, and he and his mother struggled over how to keep their practice sessions on target. They realized that setting an egg timer (for an absolute maximum of five minutes for each new practice task or measure) was the best way to keep Michael engaged with relatively complex musical content. Michael is older now, but he still relies on timers to separate his practice goals (now fifteen minutes for scales, thirty for etudes, and so on)!

Even though it's convenient to let older children use phones as timers, you can eliminate potential distractions by setting a household alarm instead (the oven timer, for example).

## It Took 1,000 Tries to Invent the Light Bulb

"Why is repetition so necessary? I'm frustrated when I can't play a new technique on the second or third try. It looks so easy when everyone else plays!" This feeling is common for beginning players. While subjects like math ask students for a correct answer on the first attempt, music demands that students refine their technique through thoughtful and deliberate repetition. To children, however, this repetition feels insulting. They would be happier if they could just play everything perfectly the first time around!

Explain to your child that persistence is valuable and mindful repetition is the secret to success. "Look, even inventing the light bulb took 1,000 tries. And light bulbs are just a few bucks! The violin (or cello, or any instrument) is so much more sophisticated. That means you are entitled to at least 1,000 tries! Keep going. You are on the right track and I love to hear you work."

## Check Your Battery

As an adult, an awareness of your own energy level helps you to remain effective as you work. Children lack this self-awareness and are unable to tell when they slip from productive practicing into foggy, distracted practicing. Teach your child how to notice how they feel—is their "focus battery" low by the time they start practice each evening? If so, it's wise to consider that feedback and schedule tomorrow's practice session for a better time. Of course, everyone has to work through fatigue at some point, but self-awareness of energy and focus aids in strategically scheduling practice to avoid this low-battery work when possible. Even better, plan activities that charge your child's focus battery (a snack with protein, a walk around the block with the dog) to keep practice sessions positive, focused, and productive.

## Move a Little!

Small and silly movements help younger children reset their focus and patience levels between repetitions. Have children set their instruments down and do a few jumping jacks or twirls whenever they start to shuffle their feet, become moody, or stop responding attentively. After a few of either exercise, even the most determined-to-be-cranky child will smile. Brief physical breaks like this extend productivity: maximize your child's ability to work effectively by keeping tabs on their energy levels in practice sessions. Ask yourself, "Is my child demonstrating low energy levels or negativity?" If so, time to move!

## Common Struggles

### Speed and Rushing

Ask any professional musician and they will confess that they, too, once struggled with rushing their tempos during practice. This tendency is extremely common and happens for a few reasons. First, whenever we (as musicians) learn to play a new piece, our brains and our fingers process the information at maximum speed—even when we play slowly, we calculate our next note as quickly as we can and play it the moment we are physically able to. When we become proficient at the piece, our bodies are still operating at that same maximum speed; this often means that each note played becomes even faster than the last. Adult musicians understand how to deal with this, but younger musicians find it difficult to separate "trying your best" from "play it as fast as you can."

The solution most teachers propose is using a metronome. In the beginning, working with the metronome frustrates both musicians and their parents: syncing up with it is just so challenging. In these cases, remember that the goal is not to merely achieve instant rhythmic success. Instead, the goal is to teach your child to partner with the metronome throughout their musical careers. Professionals are consistent with their tempos because they constantly go back to the metronome to ask, "Am I really playing in time here, or is this part so exciting musically that I unintentionally speed up?"

One of my students, Tommy, was beyond frustrated in trying to line up new passages in the Kabalevsky Violin Concerto with the metronome. "I don't understand, Ms. Haley, you're ALWAYS with the metronome. Why am I never with it?" Tommy was trying his best but losing patience. And, as he grew more frustrated, he rushed faster, further outpacing the metronome. I reassured him, "I'm playing in time with the metronome because the metronome has been my practice aid for twenty years. Tommy, you and your metronome are just getting to know each other—if you can find it within yourself to give the metronome more of a chance, it will help you."

When I was Tommy's age, I felt the same way he did. In response, my own teacher explained patiently that metronomes have no soul, and so they will always be perfectly in time. What makes us special as musicians and humans is that we DO have a soul. We get the best of all worlds by working with the metronome, learning to make deliberate tempo changes that enhance listeners' enjoyment and understanding of music.

## Not Enough Time During the Week

*"We do so well over the weekends, but by the time I come home from work during the week, we are all too worn out to make a big production out of the violin."*

How relatable is it to want to write today off and resolve to do better tomorrow, especially with something so intimidating or emotionally nuanced as practicing patiently with your child? It's always tempting to wait for another day—preferably one that doesn't come with a looming work assignment of your own. While you can sometimes plan ahead to avoid having to practice through moments of exhaustion like this, on weeknights 8 p.m. rolls around far faster than anyone anticipates.

The best solution to scheduling difficulties is to plan morning practice sessions with your child. At first though, it's pure misery. Waking up at 6 a.m. is bad enough—waking up at 5:50 a.m. seems just about impossible—besides, what's that extra ten minutes of practice really worth? Any parent can tell you how the average child will feel about practicing at that hour, as well.

However, after the first few days (or, if you are truly an anti-morning person, weeks), you and your child will begin to take pride in your early morning routine. Starting the day together in an activity that positively rewards your motivation with a boost of self-esteem will give you both more energy to conquer other intimidating tasks later in the day. You will prove to yourself and your child that yes, you really are motivated morning practicers! Even if you work together for just a few minutes before school, grabbing that victory is incredibly powerful. What a fabulous feeling to carry along with you to morning meetings—you have got your life so together that you practice violin with your child before work!

These morning practice sessions have a strong impact on performance, allowing each day to be musically successful no matter what the universe has in store for the rest of the twenty-four hours. Because early morning tends to be one of the few time windows without other extracurricular activities, it's far easier to keep this schedule when basketball season comes around.

Best of all, the world seems quieter early in the morning. Cellphones aren't ringing, news alerts aren't yet blaring, younger siblings are still sleeping, and even the yard looks prettier in the morning dew. What more could anyone want for a practice setting?

## Self-Conscious Playing

When I was in school, my classmates and I were forbidden from hanging scarves or other materials over the tiny windows in the practice room doors. At one point, the fire marshal even came by our school to put up little stickers warning us in plain language not to cover the windows. However, two days later, everyone would again be practicing behind blocked doors. We didn't want to be thought of as "the one playing the Mozart octaves over and over trying to tune them on Tuesday." We each wanted to be thought of as "the one who aced the Mozart in Saturday's performance."

Similarly, my students tell me they prefer to practice when their parents are away (or at least in another room). Practicing makes everyone feel vulnerable—working on techniques that haven't been mastered yet is a reminder to all of how much more work still needs to be done.

However, teachers assign challenging repertoire knowing full-well that it is the next playing level above a student's current abilities. When your child feels self-conscious about developing these improvements in their playing, it's tempting to accommodate their preference by becoming completely hands-off—dropping them off at lessons alone or letting them select solitary moments for their practice time.

Yet, as sensitive as children can be about being overheard practicing—similar to sharing something else of a personal nature, like their creative writing homework—parental involvement brings huge benefit. To stay involved and keep your child's insecurity at bay, remind them that you are in this with them for the long haul—squeaks or no squeaks.

> ### A Note on Siblings
>
> "She sounds bad! She didn't practice this week!" When we allow siblings to speak negatively about each other (tattle or insult), we give them musical influence that is disproportionate to their maturity. Greet these attempts with an insistent, "No talking about your sibling's playing." Valid criticism comes from parents and teachers only.

## Fatigue & Discomfort

To manage fatigue, identify whether it is physical, mental, or a combination thereof. If you can identify what causes your child to want to set down their instrument, you can find a way to help them push through.

Children in middle school doing their best work in a lesson will start to feel fatigued after about twenty minutes. Missing "silly" notes is usually the first sign. Students who lock their knees when they focus will feel exhausted even faster, sometimes fainting. Attentive teachers notice symptoms of fatigue and pace lessons accordingly. You can, too.

Ward off physical fatigue by scheduling practice sessions as early in the day as possible and making sure that meals or snacks before practice sessions contain protein. As is the case with other subjects, our brains need fuel for studying music! Children should always have water available to them in rehearsals, practice sessions, and lessons. Additionally, it's important for parents to remind young musicians about the importance of planned, scheduled practice breaks. Setting the kitchen timer helps.

Work with your child and their teacher to understand what causes fatigue or discomfort during practice and what you can do to mitigate it. For example, if a teacher insists that students stand (rather than sit) during practice, a parent might put a cushioned rug on the floor (my students swear by thick kitchen mats!) to prevent sore feet. A teacher will also point out that, for example, while the development of callouses at the tips of a string player's fingers is completely expected (stinging briefly at first), any back or wrist pain is absolutely not normal. Clear boundaries like this are crucial to helping young musicians develop a healthy awareness of their own physical well-being on the instrument.

## Practice Space

The practicality of the practice space generates the success of the time spent there. By making a few tweaks, you can solve potential practice problems before they present major issues. For example, following a teacher's exact instructions with regard to the type of practice chair (if playing a seated instrument like cello) fosters the development of proper posture and technique.

A poor choice of a chair (especially one with arms) can cause serious delay in technical development for seated players like cellists. Similarly, for standing players like violinists and violists, music stands that are set too low can quickly lead to neck and back problems and create unnecessary difficulty for shifts, vibrato, and intonation. A sturdy music stand that can easily be adjusted to the right height is a wise investment.

Another means of accelerating technical development is to install a large mirror on the wall in the practice room. Conservatories have floor-length mirrors in every practice room so musicians can keep an eye on technique and posture even while they read through new music. The mirror allows players to assess their posture accurately. If you would like to develop self-guidance in your child with regard to technique, a mirror is the most effective way to inspire this essential introspective attention to physical detail.

Some children find practicing in their bedroom unproductive. There are simply too many distractions—books to read, messages to reply to, little projects to tidy up. Working efficiently is easier in a quiet, boring room. The extra peace allows the music to be the most exciting and vibrant thing to focus on.

One of my own teachers once confessed that, as a child, he practiced scales while sitting on his bed reading comic books. The scales did not improve, but his mother was happy to hear him play them so much. He soon realized that this type of practicing didn't generate progress. Like him, I used to practice with the TV on mute, just for company. This may have made me feel less lonely during practice sessions, but my mind still went to the show first and my notes second. Discourage distractions like this, even though they may seem harmless or comforting.

## Off-Mic Comments

Have strict control over who is allowed to have a say in your child's practice sessions. As we have discussed, small, seemingly harmless remarks carry huge potential to derail your child's progress. When young players practice properly, the requisite trial-and-error process makes them feel vulnerable to stray questions like, "Ouch, can't get that note quite yet, eh?" Any parent who has made a seemingly innocuous comment during a practice session and then watched their young musician storm off in tears can relate. If grandparents and other family members want to comment, give them a few phrases to use, such as, "I love listening to you work!" "Boy, are you working well there!" "Keep playing, I'd like to stay here and listen as long as I can!" These phrases inspire confidence.

When I was about twelve years old, my family invited a few relatives to visit. To celebrate the occasion, my brother and I performed for everyone. Later in the evening, I overheard one relative in the room adjoining mine say, "Lauren likes playing all right, but that Nathan, he's got it in his *soul*." I took it to mean that my little brother's talent so far exceeded my own that everyone in the room could see the disparity, even though none of my relatives had ever played so much as one note themselves.

I let that mindset hinder my practicing for a month. I felt that if I was seen trying too hard (by continuing to diligently practice), I was making a fool out of myself. Instead, I wanted everyone to know that I was in on the joke—see, I too knew I shouldn't take music too seriously, since that was clearly my younger brother's job!

It wasn't until I told my mother about the overheard comment that I realized how completely incorrect it was and how foolish I had been to let it derail me. Even in later years, though, when my brother and I performed in competitions (often against each other), this negative the comment replayed in my head. The tiny bit of truth I saw in it still felt powerful and destructive years later.

Adult students, picking up their violin for the first time in twenty years, often tell me it was an "off-mic" comment like this that convinced them to give up music as children. I can relate—in my own twelve-year-old mind, I too had briefly let an acknowledgment of my brother's talent make my own playing feel less worthy of pursuit.

## I'll Do It Later

Saying, "I'll do it later," is usually an act of unrealistic optimism for anyone who wants to delay addressing a difficult or dreaded task. Most children do honestly believe they will finish the work later.

They don't have a lifetime of experience with consequences of procrastination in the way that we do as adults.

So, of course, given that many children truly intend to practice (just, you know, later), when parents come in and say, "I can't believe you're not practicing! Do you not want this (goal) badly enough?! Are you just lazy?!" children feel insulted and put off. Their latent fear of being called out comes to life, and they more strongly resist practicing as a result.

Given that practicing means confronting the difficulties in any given piece, getting to work is intimidating when children are unsure of how to approach any new content or have fuzzy memories of the last lesson. In their youthful optimism, they truly believe they will confront the obstacles...later. The common thread is that young musicians think they will be able to practice well if they just put off that confrontation until some arbitrary time in the future.

The best thing to do here is simply remind children that they don't have to know all the answers at the beginning of a practice session. All they have to do is open the case and get started.

# Chapter 6

---

# Obstacles Create High Achievers

*"We've been really trying for the last few weeks, but it's one struggle after another. I'm afraid Kelly is just not talented. Learning to play viola is really hard—beautiful sound doesn't come naturally at all. It looks so easy for her friend Joe when he plays, and I never see his parents argue with him over practicing! Maybe we should try something else, like sports—what do you think? Does Kelly just not have what it takes to pursue music?"*

AS FAMILIES STRIVE for musical excellence, obstacles inevitably appear in the path. Conquering these obstacles (music-based, logistical, or personal) enables children to become better versions of themselves. Dealing with obstacles is absolutely essential to growth and the further development of resilience and perseverance.

The violin, for example, has a reputation for being the most challenging instrument to master. Still, it's one of the most expressive and rewarding to play. The many difficulties it offers can seem so troubling and overwhelming at times that young musicians and their parents might decide music must not be for them. Some parents remember similar frustrations from their own studies, and that memory influences their desire to protect their child.

Pulling the plug on musical study in the face of difficulties is like selling stock at an all-time low. When you do so, you lock in the losses. If you let your child quit their studies when their musical path feels rocky, they lose their musical potential. Further, quitting risks validating a young musician's perception that they should be talented at any pursuit before it's worth their effort.

Instead, the best time to invest in your child's musical ability is when they require that extra support. By providing additional emotional and strategic musical support at these times, you invest effectively in your child's ability to grow and you contribute positively to their future success. The key is to remember that every musician (without exception) has faced challenges. Recognize the obstacles in your child's path for what they truly are—growth opportunities in disguise.

## Growth Obstacles

Some obstacles appear to be true hindrances but are merely temporary inconveniences with valuable skills to teach. We see this type of obstacle all the time in pop culture, especially on children's TV shows, where the characters must solve some dilemma or learn the moral of the story at the end of each episode. Still, it's hard to recognize growth obstacles in the context of music lessons. Young musicians would rather just develop the new technique or sound their teacher wants and skip the musical moral of the story.

An example of an unanticipated growth obstacle might be working with a difficult partner on an upcoming duet performance. That experience might lead a child to develop in ways that the original project itself did not set out to do. In this case, the obstacle (collaborating with the difficult partner) would develop their collaboration skills. Another growth obstacle might be a teacher's insistence that a child perform in public for the first time. The child may not yet feel brave enough, but the teacher gives the challenge of an upcoming performance to develop the child's confidence. In both cases, it might be tempting to intervene to make things easier for the child ("Let's wait another year to have his first performance."), but that action would be counterproductive to long-term growth. In short, removing growth obstacles might relieve short-term struggle for your child, but this action fails to foster growth in the long term.

## Hindrance Obstacles

By contrast, hindrance obstacles tend to be unintentional matters of circumstance. For example, missing one lesson per month when the lesson conflicts with soccer would be an unnecessary hindrance obstacle—it would be far better to simply switch soccer teams or lesson days. Another example might be an instrument that is one size too large for a child. The poorly sized instrument would hinder the true goal of technical development. Obstacles like these are not deliberate challenges given to further a child's development, just haphazard inconveniences that make musical study more difficult than necessary. In cases like this, resolving the obstacle moves children forward both in the short term and in the long term.

| Growth Obstacles Are | Hindrance Obstacles Are |
|---|---|
| Challenges that make us better (more efficient, determined, or skilled). | Accidental matters of circumstance. |
| Purposeful and are given by teachers and parents. | Difficulties that stall rather than spur personal or musical development. |
| Necessary for development. It's the job of the child (not parents or teachers) to solve them. | Easily resolved by the adults in a child's life. |

## Obstacles and Emotional Development

Until the start of kindergarten, parents are in charge of the obstacles their children face. Toys and games start out simple, and each new skill is celebrated as a milestone—the first smile, first words, first steps. When each achievement is so obviously a source of joy, conquering new obstacles comes naturally.

As children transition into school, teachers determine the academic obstacles. Even when the assignments seem easy to adults, each one is new and significant when faced for the very first time and carries the goal of furthering the student's emotional and academic development.

---

### External vs. Internal Obstacles

When you identify the source of an obstacle as external or internal you can address the true challenge at hand. Determine which obstacles come from your child (temper tantrums, learned helplessness, procrastination) and you (schedule conflicts, lesson tardiness) and which challenges instead come from outside sources (situations, assignments, deadlines). Begin by addressing the issues over which you have the most control.

---

## Fixable vs. Manageable Obstacles

Obstacles are present throughout development and life—like it or not, we are all given our own challenges. Whether these difficulties fall within our control or outside of it, having an awareness of obstacles as catalysts for developing strength helps us as teachers and parents foster that growth in children.

The obstacles that we cannot fix, but can learn how to manage, teach this the best. For example, your child's school orchestra program may be lackluster—you, as the parent, are not in a position to resolve this situation. You can, however, supplement school orchestra participation with a private youth orchestra experience for your child. In situations like this, ask yourself, "Even if I can't fix this, how can I best manage it?"

## Age-Specific Challenges

### Ages 3–5

For this age group, parents have control over most of the challenges and obstacles children encounter. Most are presented joyfully, and each new accomplishment is celebrated with hugs, smiles, and kisses.

Who wouldn't want to learn to walk, read, or spell when each bit of progress brings so much joy? When a three-year-old begins studying music, some challenges fall outside the realm of parental control. The study of a stringed instrument like the violin presents innate physical difficulties. When this happens, musical challenges seem daunting, certainly outpacing the difficulty level of academic tasks in children's pre-K studies.

The remedy for this is simple: celebrate absolutely every learning victory, no matter how tiny. For students ages three through five, it's crucial for parents to engage with every moment of the lesson. It's so easy to miss the one note that your child has finally played with a straight bow when you are glancing at your phone. Distractions in lessons rob you and your child of the happiness each new accomplishment brings.

## Elementary and Middle School

As children work their way through elementary and middle school, their teachers (both at school and in private lessons) present obstacles. Learning opportunities like orchestra competitions may be organized by regional or statewide programs. Private lessons allow students to learn at their own best pace, focusing on just the right challenge at the right time. Evaluate the way your child's music teacher sets appropriate musical obstacles and conduct honest conversations with them about each week's progress. Consider that some teachers find it easy to slip into a lax routine, minimizing the pace of presented obstacles (and progress) in order to avoid conflicts over the work being accomplished between lessons.

### High School

In high school, young musicians should be aware of how obstacles interact with their use of time each day. As high-school students learn time management, they begin to understand the difference between prioritizing ("This task is the best use of my time right now.") and procrastination ("I'll have time to write my paper and practice later, so I can watch one episode now!"). Teaching teenagers how to prioritize is more helpful than simply advising them not to procrastinate.

## The Biggest Obstacle: Feeling Overwhelmed

When is too much really just too much? How do you know when a child's resistance to practicing or learning the instrument is more than just a phase? After all, even professional musicians confess that they, too, had moments as children when they refused to practice. At what point is it unhealthy to insist that the child play the instrument, despite the family fights and shouting? Is it ever wise to take a break from the instrument for a few months or years to let the child mature?

Make a list of the difficulties and frustrations you and your child face. Write down issues or concerns you have about the teacher, the instrument, the difficulty in finding time to practice, the challenges of establishing a daily practice routine, the way other school subjects or work commitments get in your way. Write down how you feel each time you tell your child something they already have been told in their lessons. Write about how worried you are when practice sessions dissolve into tears after only a few minutes. If you like, ask your spouse or child to make a similar list. The first step to defeating overwhelm is simply writing down your family's feelings.

Next, assign categories to each difficulty as follows. Some obstacles are emotion-based (frustration), some are technical (holding the instrument properly), some are academic (school orchestra grades), some are logistics-based (instrument quality), some are social ("All of my friends play sports!"), and some are due to scheduling (for example, the sports coach calls last-minute team meets that overlap with lessons). Assigning categories lets your family see the root cause of struggles.

Divide your categories into two subsets: predictable struggles and unexpected challenges. For example, attending regular lessons after 9 p.m. on weeknights can be expected to present unnecessary difficulty for younger students—unfocused playing and grumpy behavior will come as no surprise. The same goes for practicing: if a parent would really like to establish a practice routine, but regularly schedules sessions for 8 p.m., they might find that the late hour makes productive work far more difficult than necessary. Do your best to limit routine-based difficulties like this.

The next category involves unexpected obstacles. This encompasses everything from the make-up soccer game that conflicts with a lesson to becoming ill the night before an audition. Look ahead to surprises like this and plan how your family might manage or avoid them.

No matter how well anyone plans, unexpected things come up. To prevent feelings of overwhelm in such cases, teachers advise students to begin music assignments on the day the assignment is given. It's far wiser to commence work based on an assignment's given date rather than its deadline. This mindset works well not just because children remember goals better when they have just agreed to them, but also because it's impossible to know if or when urgent priorities might pop up before a deadline.

Here's an illustration of how this approach, of always preparing far in advance of deadlines, really works: In the weeks leading up to a local competition, one of my students, Melissa, had prepared exceptionally well. She had attended extra lessons, followed her practice routine, and studied the music carefully. Then, the day before the competition, Melissa developed food poisoning. She was totally unable to practice that day, a day on which most of her competitors were putting in highly intense, if last-minute, efforts. Had Melissa not prepared so well over the previous weeks, the missed practice would have seriously affected her ability to perform well. However, because of her top-notch preparation in the weeks leading to the competition, the one-day muscle memory loss barely affected her performance; she aced it. Like Melissa, your child can handle unexpected obstacles well by letting good habits guide progress in the long term.

## Emotion-Based Obstacles

Children aren't always able to identify or communicate effectively about the obstacles they are really facing—feelings of frustration over sound quality, self-doubt regarding whether or not they have talent, or fear that their practicing will fail to advance their playing. Given that motivation comes from feeling that their efforts create meaningful improvement, hopelessness and self-doubt are tricky obstacles to overcome. When you sense that your child is struggling with insecurities like this, the best approach is to consistently talk with their teacher to evaluate how you can effectively guide your child through home practice as they mature.

On the flip side, observe your child's lessons—is the way the teacher speaks spurring your child on through picky but constructive criticism? If, by contrast, you detect the slightest hint of belittling behavior, with negative engagements in lessons, your child's teacher may be contributing to these feelings of hopelessness. We will discuss teachers further in Chapter 7.

## Technical Obstacles

A technical obstacle is a desired ability on the instrument that has not yet been achieved. Repeated difficulty in overcoming technical musical obstacles can make it seem to a young musician that they are "just not talented." There are three ways to proceed here.

The first is to consult with the teacher, who can advise on the physical source of difficulty. For example, on the violin, developing a proper bow hold takes incredible persistence and attention to detail for students and parents. That can be overwhelming, especially because it looks so easy when professionals and advanced students, with thousands of hours of practice under their belts, perform. Your child's teacher can assure that this proficiency will come, given time and consistent effort.

The second way to proceed is to honestly evaluate how regular your child's practice sessions are. Instrumental technique development requires muscle and sensory memory, both of which can only be developed through deliberate and consistent daily repetition. For example, if a student knows in their mind how to do vibrato, but is unable to correctly perform the physical motion when they play, they become frustrated. They rationalize this difference between what they know how to do mentally, but cannot do physically, by concluding that they are untalented.

If this is confusing, think of it this way—you may know how to run twenty-six miles (simply put one leg in front of the other and keep going), but unless you train for it, running that marathon is going to be extremely difficult, if even possible. Muscle and sensory memory development is similar to athletic development. Each day, the body either becomes more advanced or lets the muscle memory deteriorate. If your child practices only every other day, putting in quite a bit of time but leaving too many days off, they will most likely experience unnecessary frustration.

The third way is to emphasize the indispensable value of repetition in each practice session and lesson. When students are taught new techniques on the instrument, they would like to be able to perform them physically as soon as they comprehend the required motions. However, technique development commonly requires work on some small task daily for weeks before the new skill can be taken for granted. This differs wildly from subjects like math, in which getting the right answer the first time through a problem is not just rewarded, but also expected. Students, used to that type of learning, struggle to justify their playing when they find they must strive through many repetitions before finally achieving the desired results. To make matters worse, when parents express frustration to a child who lets their bow hold slip or elbow fall long after they have been taught the right way, parents risk accidentally implying that something must be wrong with the child's ability to learn. By contrast, when a teacher tells a student to correct their posture, and later it needs correcting again, the teacher understands that this is not necessarily a deliberate failing on part of the student. Modifying muscle memory is more similar to how, for example, you might know you are not supposed to bite your nails and decide to cut the habit. The next day at work you might look down at your hands and realize you have just broken your own resolution. This setback would not imply that you should give up, it would just mean that long-term effort is required to change any physical habit.

## Academic Obstacles

There is a misperception that playing music will take time or effort away from other academics. Some parents worry that if their child spends considerable time practicing daily, other subjects will slip. If this were truly the case, Ivy League orchestra enrollment would be far lower than it actually is. Instead, there is a high correlation between musical proficiency and success in other areas of study. In addition to the artistic value of performance, the study of music also teaches its followers how to be better learners.

However, there is one way in which studying music can, actually, be damaging to other school subjects and vice versa. When students do not practice daily, they find that they need to cram practicing into the day before the school chair test or competition. This three hours of practicing the night before a deadline is frustrating and, because it takes up the whole evening, definitely puts a damper on studying any other subjects that night. If this situation occurs every week on Thursday night before the Friday chair test, then other Friday subjects and tests will absolutely suffer. Students feel forced to choose—cram math or cram violin? Often, math wins because music is usually an elective, not a core subject. With sloppy planning like this, academics become obstacles to musical achievement and both avenues of study falter.

Additionally, when students are not appropriately supported on their instrument (for example, they are the only student who does not have a private teacher in a class of students who do), attaining musical proficiency will be more time-consuming than it would be for their classmates. Parents sometimes argue that they do not want to commit their child to an hour lesson each week, but the child ends up spending far more than just that hour in extra practice time because they do not have the professional guidance their peers do. Notes and techniques are learned more efficiently when a child is coached one-on-one by a professional.

Families who successfully balance high-level music and academics agree upon a time-specific daily practice routine that fits with their lifestyle. Practice time is not subject to, "Well, as long as I have no tests tomorrow," or "I'll practice whenever I finish the rest of my homework—if I still have energy by then." Instead, it's just part of what the child does each day. This is similar to how adults don't tell children that the thirty minutes they spend getting ready each morning take time away from studying. Instead, that time is just built into the daily routine. Apply the same approach to musical study.

Valuable lessons and learning strategies will spill over from practice time into students' academic lives. Committing to musical self-improvement for thirty minutes per day (for example) gives students a framework through which they learn how to self-direct the rest of their studies. For those who practice as soon as they get home from school, it helps them transition from frazzled to focused and creates the right mindset for homework. It also provides comfort, control, and routine even through the daily variations and challenges that school and family life bring.

## Logistical Obstacles

Logistical obstacles involve issues like lacking consistent transportation to and from lessons, being unable able to carry the instrument home each day from school, or even just acquiring an appropriate instrument to begin with. Logistical obstacles usually fall outside the realm of student responsibility and are best addressed by parents and teachers. Logistical obstacles are overwhelming when they pile up, but many are simple to solve when adults stop to examine the situation more closely and prioritize efficiently.

I recently enrolled a new family in my studio, a violinist named Christina and her father, Kevin. Kevin was excited for Christina to finally be off the waiting list and into the studio. However, when Christina got off the bus the day of her first lesson with me, she didn't have her instrument—she had left it at school. Kevin was upset that they would be attending their first lesson without Christina's violin. When they brought Christina's violin to the following week's lesson, I saw immediately why Christina had the habit of leaving it at school. The shop had given her a viola case, not a violin case, and it was far too heavy for a child Christina's size to carry in addition to her backpack. I too would have left that cumbersome thing at school! It was an easy fix—the family was renting the violin from a local shop that should certainly should have given Christina an appropriate case to begin with. When Kevin and Christina went back to the shop, the case was of course exchanged free of charge. When Christina finally had an appropriate, lightweight case, she didn't mind carrying it home from school every day.

These kinds of things seem like simple changes, but it's surprising how many self-professed "serious" musical families end up with a defective instrument or poorly sized case just because their local music shop happened to be out of what they needed on a particular day. Rather than mentioning this stock issue to customers, shops sometimes just sell whatever happens to be available that day. Parents, especially those encountering an instrument for the first time, often don't notice the difference. The best course of action here is to communicate with your child's teacher about how adjustments in "music gear" might make things easier or more efficient for your child.

## Social Obstacles

*"If Jess gets into the first violin section, I'm quitting the class. She doesn't belong here with us." "I don't think Calvin deserves to be first chair. He's squeaky. And ugly."*

Kids can be mean, and it's important to learn from each instance rather than let it negatively impact a child's relationship with the instrument. When children perceive that their participation in music makes them look foolish to their peers, they are less likely to be proud of the effort it takes to excel.

When I was auditioning for music schools, a friend, Joe, told me that our mutual friend, Chris, said I was a horrible violinist. Chris had told Joe that if I were accepted into Chris's teacher's studio at the conservatory, he would leave the school in protest. I was upset—this seemed to validate my own insecurities, and right before my big audition for that school, too! I confided in my teacher what I'd heard. She listened patiently, then looked me in the eyes and asked, "This Chris kid—he's a freshman? At the conservatory?" I said yes. She laughed. "Freshmen don't know anything, trust me. You don't even know if Chris is going to make it all the way through the four years—things don't look good for him if he's bashing incoming students. Don't listen to him. Listen to your teachers and your parents. Also, you might want to question your friendship with Joe if he's repeating things like that to you. He's not pushing you forward either."

Bullying happens, and we can't make any subject or instrument bully proof. Strategic parenting here means keeping teachers up to date on what's really going on in a child's social life. The consequences of bullying are becoming more widely recognized, and more resources are available to parents each year. Parents can also work with teachers and school counselors to address this issue.

On a similar note, students have confessed to me that they are intimidated by another student at school or in the studio. "I'll never be first chair—Kathy is always, always first. It doesn't matter how much I practice, I won't catch up. She's just better than me." To children, this close competition with other players feels like their whole musical world. Remind your child that if they find themselves motivated by competitors, that's great. On the other hand, if they reduce the purpose of their study to just being the best in school, winning certain events, or playing the hardest piece at recitals, they might struggle later when it comes time to compete on a national or international level. Tell your child to compete against their own best selves first, and everyone else second.

---

### Evaluate Obstacles

Regularly running into challenges will teach you and your child how to manage these difficulties. Clarify obstacles and establish positive paths forward by asking these questions:

Is this obstacle helping or hurting my child in the short term?
Is it contributing or hindering long-term growth or happiness?
Is there a bigger purpose to having this obstacle in our lives?
What factors here are outside my control as the parent?
Is there someone else whose help we could enlist?

---

## The Takeaway

The violin's job is to generate problems. Your child's task is to solve these problems. Your mission is to "edit" the problems—determine which ones help your child advance (a strict teacher, a difficult new piece) and which ones hinder your child's development (scheduling conflicts, an inappropriately-sized instrument). Obstacles are effective teachers because appropriate short-term inconveniences or frustrations can develop long-term perseverance and resilience.

We can't control or even predict every obstacle and (for better or worse) we can't solve them all, either. Instead, our task is to harness music to teach children how to recognize and approach the challenges that will shape their life—musically, academically, and personally—in the future. We do this by keeping the lines of communication open between students, parents, and teachers, and generating solutions.

# Chapter 7

## Invest in Teachers and Instruments

### Finding Your Best Instructor

The most common mistake parents of young musicians make is selecting a low-quality teacher when their child begins a new instrument. Musicians' credentials are difficult to decode for non-musicians, private lessons seem hugely expensive compared to other age-appropriate activities, and the world's littlest violinist doesn't always look like he would benefit fully from a top-notch teacher.

In reality, investing too little effort in finding a quality teacher limits your child's potential. After all, who has more potential than those who are only three years old and already starting to explore music? Moreover, lessons are far less efficient with under-qualified teachers. A low-quality teacher over time is far more expensive than an effective teacher is in covering the same amount of material. Worse still, these teachers might never cover the material their well-qualified competitors will. Additionally, pursuing an instrument for a lifetime without injury requires excellent technique. Teachers with mediocre credentials often are not aware of the flaws in their technique.

Appropriate technique is especially important for string players, vocalists, and pianists. String players and pianists practice the highest number of hours throughout their lifetimes (often from age three!), and effective technique provides the best chance to avoid tension-based injury for as long as possible. Vocalists' technique is hugely significant as well due to the way the human voice develops. An unskilled vocal teacher can damage a student's voice for life by pushing them into inappropriately heavy repertoire at a young age. While there may be slightly less risk of injury for wind and brass players, who often don't start their instruments until fifth or sixth grade and are more limited in the number of hours per day they can play, the preferable route always is to start with the best available instructor.

Keep in mind that working with a teacher whose coaching style does not mesh well with the family often results in children quitting their instrument. When this happens, families blame themselves, unaware of the difference a better student-teacher match would make. The unfortunate result is that the child is denied the emotional and social growth benefits a musical education should include. This situation also sets up a dislike for musical study.

## Evaluating Appropriate Teachers

First, consider degrees. B.M. (Bachelor of Music), M.M. (Master of Music), and D.M.A. (Doctoral of Musical Arts) degrees all imply serious musical training. B.A., M.A., and Ph.D. programs can represent a lower level of instrumental performance, but are typical for those pursuing music theory and history.

A conservatory degree means that a musician's education took place at a school focused on the arts, as opposed to a general university that offers music degrees in addition to a broad range of other subjects. While the rankings of conservatories vary by year, top performers are awarded degrees from schools like Juilliard, the Eastman School of Music, the Curtis Institute of Music, and the

New England Conservatory, just to name a few of the very best in the United States.

A conservatory education also means that a musician's primary course of study was music. Standard subjects are usually replaced with their specialized musical equivalents (music theory instead of math, music history instead of world history) to lead to the highest level of musical proficiency.

## Applied Music vs. Music Education

A degree in Applied Music in a specific instrument is a degree that specializes in the performance of that instrument. A degree in Music Education often means the degree required proficiency on several instruments, which is ideal for teaching orchestra and band in middle and secondary schools.

## Primary vs. Secondary Instruments

Consider whether the instrument your child is pursuing is the teacher's own primary instrument. A graduate in tuba performance is typically less ideal as a piano teacher than a professional pianist would be, even though the tuba player may have studied piano as part of their degree's standard curriculum. Musicians in conservatories are usually required to spend a few years studying piano as part of their degree (regardless of their primary instrument), but this does not mean that they will have received specific training in creating paths for their own students to develop into proficient pianists. If you want to open musical doors for your child, pair them with an appropriate instrumentalist from their earliest lessons.

## Professional Engagements

Lastly, evaluate potential instructors' post-degree careers, including professional engagements. Do they perform in a professional symphony or an amateur one? Professional symphonies (New York Philharmonic, Houston Symphony Orchestra, and many others) hold competitive auditions that go for several rounds. Musicians travel from all over the world to compete for a spot. Amateur symphonies are far less competitive, usually do not pay a salary, and draw from local musicians who have pursued non-performance careers professionally.

Consider that teachers who do not continually play or practice advanced repertoire lose their muscle memory, making them less able to perform advanced technique in lessons. This is one reason why conservatory and college music professors are usually required to perform yearly recitals. If you want your child to be able to play the Tchaikovsky Violin Concerto, you must hire a teacher who engages with that level of repertoire in their own musical life. Of course, there are some exceptions—including incredible lifelong musicians who may have stopped performing due to age or disability—who still offer invaluable experience to their students.

## Teaching Studios

Teachers who put in heavy practice or performance hours usually refrain from driving to clients' houses for lessons: it's not a productive use of their time. While young teachers, who may not yet have a studio suitable for lessons, may drive to clients' homes, this setup can also indicate low demand for a particular teacher's time.

On the flip side, by being unwilling to drive to teachers' studios for their children's lessons, some families may be demonstrating that they are not ready to invest time and energy into those lessons.

In-demand teachers observe this and, as a result, avoid accepting families who insist that the teacher come to the family's home.

Think carefully before selecting a teacher who teaches at a chain music store. While these arrangements may be helpful initially in connecting instrument purchasers with teachers, typically, teachers keep only a percentage of the lesson fee. High-level teachers understand the value of their time and avoid this or move to establish their own studio as quickly as possible. Also, chain music stores frequently do not employ personnel with the expertise to effectively manage or control the quality of the teachers they hire. All of the above typically lead to high turnover in both students and teachers. Lastly, be aware that teachers who advertise on websites like Craigslist and Thumbtack may do so because they do not attract enough clients through referrals and personal recommendations.

## Personality

Highly nuanced musical communication on the part of the teacher is a key determinant of progress in lessons, whether or not the teacher is an acclaimed performer. No matter how advanced a performer may be, the ability to communicate effectively at your child's maturity level is crucial: "Just play it like I do," is unhelpful advice. For example, a renowned $300-per-hour conservatory professor may seem like the best instructor available, but if they are not familiar with the learning obstacles your child's current age group presents, they may not be an effective teacher for your family.

Would-be performers who actually prefer not to teach and only do so for the extra income are to be avoided. Your child's teacher should want to be in your child's lessons as much as you do.

## Lesson Length and Frequency

For younger students and beginners, frequent (and short) lessons facilitate increased ease on the instrument and speed up the learning process. For the youngest beginners (ages three to five), shorter lessons mean students will stop playing before they feel fatigued and frustrated. Lessons end with the student still wanting to learn more—what a great way to develop enthusiasm, anticipation, and motivation for music right from the beginning! It is well worth the extra drive to attend two short lessons per week with this age group instead of just one longer lesson.

For all age groups, attending lessons frequently (twice per week instead of once) allows students to retain complex information and technique better. Frequent reinforcement boosts productivity immensely—it truly is the most efficient way to improve. Even advanced young musicians find that they quadruple their learning speed when lessons are held twice each week instead of once.

For advanced students, lesson length should depend on the child's repertoire, goals, and ability to focus for long stretches of time. While hour lessons are often standard, ninety-minute lessons (with a short break in the middle) help students cover a vast amount of repertoire and technique.

Remember that the more time your child spends in lesson with their teacher, the more thoroughly their teacher is able to cover each week's material. In this sense, taking hour lessons each week instead of forty-five-minute lessons means your child will likely have a much easier time at home practicing.

Private lessons are most effective when they occur at least once per week on a regular basis. Musical momentum is nearly impossible to maintain if lessons are only every fourteen days. Frequent reinforcement here truly is the key to success, and putting too many days between lessons will severely limit lesson effectiveness and make home practice unnecessarily difficult.

If your child studies with a performer who travels frequently for concerts, address this added challenge. Teachers who have your child's best interests at heart will recommend a colleague to coach your child through missed weeks.

---

### Questions to Consider

- Is the teacher recommended by or currently associated with local musicians, families, schools, and youth organizations?
- Do other students in the studio share your family's musical goals?
- Does the teacher's studio target your child's age group?
- Does the teacher still actively perform? Did they pursue—at one point—a career in a professional symphony or ensemble?
- Do the teacher's location and hours suit your availability?

---

## When to Fire a Teacher

It can be hard to tell when a teacher crosses the line from being an effective coach to being ineffective or downright harmful. Here are some signs.

Consider whether the teacher is consistently passive, cynical, or exhibiting low energy. Moods are contagious, and teachers who dislike their careers may pass the attitude on to students. While it may seem worthwhile to have a famous teacher who just happens to be cranky, how much more effective could an equally brilliant teacher with positive energy be?

It's wise to move on from teachers who start their lessons late and/or end early when this denies your child their full lesson time on a regular basis. Issues like this make it harder to maximize each week's instruction and may send the message that the teacher has more important things to do with their time than to help students. Similarly, avoid teachers who are distracted during lessons—routine cooking, texting, phone calls, or paperwork demonstrate an inability to focus on musical development. Multitasking may appear efficient and effective, but it's a huge loss in terms of focused learning.

Additionally, unclear verbal communication from teachers may translate to frustration at home during practice. You can clarify your child's comprehension of each lesson by discussing the lesson material together during the car ride home from each class, but when a teacher's communication style poses a significant extra difficulty and misunderstandings over assignments lead to confrontations, it may be better to switch teachers.

Consider moving on from teachers who under-emphasize technique. For example, "We never play scales—those aren't fun enough." If it's difficult to accurately evaluate a teacher's proficiency on an instrument, allow the emphasis they place on technique in lesson to be the guide. Teachers should emphasize form and function—be wary of those who rarely mention it. This emphasis flips at the very highest level, after students have gained a solid technical basis. At that point, teachers will focus primarily on musicality and interpretation, using technique as a vehicle for artistic elements.

Avoid teachers who create no concrete steps toward goals for your child. Lesson focus should be not just on results but also on specific how to's and here's-what-we-learned-here moments. For example, teachers with large studios and busy performing careers might forget which techniques they have already covered for a particular student. Their students may go along with the charade to have an easier lesson that week. This shortcoming weakens a teacher's ability to create short- and long-term goals for their students. Otherwise outstanding teachers may be afforded a few memory lapses, but the best teachers systematically keep track of their students' progress and goals.

In evaluating a teacher's ability to set appropriate goals for your child, consider whether the teacher uses repertoire promises to bounce back from lessons that involved tears or shouting. For example, using exciting future repertoire as a tease without putting forth a disciplined path to get there can indicate that a teacher just wants the student to keep going—and for parents to keep paying tuition—regardless of the student's actual anticipated progress. It's best to move on from teachers who set goals in this way.

While teachers at advanced levels may expect students to find their own competitions, performances, and recitals, teachers for young students or beginners should help parents find performance opportunities by putting on studio recitals and identifying local performance opportunities (for example, performing holiday music at a mall or assisted living center).

At the end of the day, a teacher's primary focus should be your child's musical growth. Avoid lesson environments based on hero worship (adoration for a prestigious teacher without regard to their actual treatment of students) and be aware of how impactful any particular teacher can be to your child's progress.

---

### Major Red Flags

**Physical Intimidation**
- Throwing or breaking pencils, music, or stands

**Verbal Abuse**
- Name-calling ("Idiot! Play in tune!")
- Raised voice
- Labeling ("Stop being so mediocre!")

***Any action or gesture on the part of the teacher that is perceived as threatening by the child is unacceptable.***

---

## How to Fire a Teacher

First, check the teacher's policy on appropriate notice and whether there is the potential for dispute over any pre-paid tuition. If any of the major red flags listed above are present, immediate dismissal for your child's sake is more urgent than getting your money back from the last few lessons of the month.

The music world is small, so handle your search for a new teacher with discretion. Avoid bad-mouthing your current teacher; it's worth handling the separation as politely as possible. In a few years, the teacher you are firing could be the conductor of your child's youth orchestra or on the jury of a local competition. Let your relationship with them remain positive.

Thank the teacher for your time together. Even though your family is ready to move on to a new instructor, you and your child have grown together musically in part because of your teacher's work over the years. Using an appropriate medium, such as a phone call or private in-person meeting, for this last communication is important. Texts and emails are considered a disrespectful way to end lessons.

## Invest Appropriately in Instruments

*"It's such a big commitment! Is there any real difference, other than the price? Our family isn't musical; the instrument options all look and sound the same. We'd like to wait a few months and see if Kayleigh is talented and still motivated to practice before spending that kind of money."*

It is vital to invest in an appropriate instrument at every stage. As a teacher and professional musician, let me testify that the most debilitating thing a child can be given early on in their study is a badly made instrument. Exceptionally cheap "starter instruments" are legitimately unplayable. Because the instrument itself has no potential, the child's potential talent is wasted as well. Rather than waiting for your child to prove to you that they have motivation or innate talent before procuring a decent instrument, let the instrument help your child acquire both of these gifts. Have confidence as you start this journey—your child's hands are as perfectly formed and ready to play music as anyone else's are and your child deserves a worthy instrument that reflects the value of their efforts.

A musical instrument is a tool with a purpose. If it cannot perform its purpose well, it might as well be hung on the wall. Given that sound is a function of physics, the physical construction of an instrument has huge sway in determining the quality of sound a young musician will produce.

Interestingly, instruments that are slightly more expensive to rent or buy are often less costly to maintain. For example, a $60 violin from Craigslist may seem like a deal, but it could require $500 in modifications and repairs before it would function well. Avoid procuring instruments like these or any instrument that would be difficult to return for any reason whatsoever. You are much better off investing in a quality instrument from the start that won't require extensive repair or maintenance.

## How to Invest in a Proper Instrument: Renting vs. Buying

### When to Rent

In the early and intermediate stages of learning an instrument, many parents choose to rent. Renting is ideal for beginners because growing children need to upsize their instrument frequently. With rentals, children may trade in small instruments for larger ones when needed. Parents don't have to worry about selling the old one before buying a new one.

Families new to music may not yet be able to perform string changes or other minor maintenance on the instrument. For rental instruments, all such repairs and small services are provided by the store. Additionally, most shops offer insurance for rentals, easing potential concerns about damage from small mishaps as families become used to handling and holding the instrument properly.

String instruments often improve in terms of tone quality when they have been played constantly. This means a rental instrument valued at $900 could potentially sound and play better than a new $900 instrument for purchase, just because it has been played so much. Ask your teacher for guidance in finding these gems in a store's rental fleet.

## What to Look for When Renting

The first thing to look for when you are ready to rent an instrument for your child is a shop that specializes in the appropriate section of the orchestra. For example, if your child wishes to play violin, rent from a shop that has luthiers (string instrument makers) on-site. If your child wishes to pursue trumpet, rent from a shop that specializes in brass instruments. Shops that do not have trained staff on-site to maintain your instrument will ship it out for repairs, costing your child days of lost practice time.

Look for shops that offer rent-to-own instrument policy options. With this type of rental contract, the monthly rental fee builds equity at the shop. At the end of a predetermined amount of time under these arrangements, a portion of the paid-in value of the instrument can be applied toward a more expensive for-purchase instrument at the same shop.

Because of this, select your child's instrument from a shop that carries a wide price range. It may not feel like you need to rent from the shop that carries $5,000 instruments in the first years of study, but when your young violinist is several years older and you have built up $2,000 of credit at the shop you will want that equity to be at a store that can offer you a superior instrument for your advancing musician.

## When to Buy

It's time to buy when the caliber of instrument your child needs is unavailable through rental programs. This is fabulous news! Purchasing an advanced instrument will allow your child to create entirely new levels of tone quality and nuance. High-quality instruments are easier to play, too. This facilitates the development of advanced technique.

Another sign that it's time to buy is the prospect of upcoming competitions—when awards, scholarships, and important school grades are on the line, choose the best available (yet affordable) option to give your child every advantage. Your teacher can help your family compare instruments in different price ranges. Remember, you're looking for an instrument that will allow for musical growth over the course of several years.

Many families choose to buy when their child is able to play a full-size instrument, often around the first year of high school. Advanced students will most likely need to purchase a quality instrument sooner. If it's affordable for your family, do so as soon as you know your child is serious about music. Advanced instruments truly do open up doors to new levels of playing. The best race car driver will have a tough time winning competitions on horseback, and the same is true for music competitions. Procuring the best possible instrument provides huge advantages. Talk to your teacher about how to do this strategically on your family's budget.

Buying is also a great choice for families with multiple children who will use the same instrument size over several years. Do the pricing math on buying versus renting for multiple siblings to arrive at the right decision for your family.

### Finding the Right Store

The store you purchase your instrument from matters greatly. It should be able to provide maintenance and repairs on-site and without excessive delay. Buy only from a specialist in your section (brass, strings, piano). String players, buy only from a luthier, even if the shop is farther away from home than a generic music store. The people at your chosen shop must be able to handle all repairs on-site.

Appropriate shops also have instrument specialists and players on hand to help you choose the right instrument. For example, a violinist at the store may play for you on a few instruments and guide you in listening for the best one. High-quality stores seek out performers for staff for this very purpose. Because of the highly competitive nature of the business, the cost of renting and purchasing instruments from these stores is close to the cost of procuring an instrument from a lower-tier shop. Avoid all-purpose music stores that sell everything from guitars to trumpets to violas. These shops are often unable to offer an appropriate range of quality and service for serious music students.

Because the instrument's ability to function is so crucial, shops should be ready to provide appropriate support when instruments need maintenance. Good shops offer loaner instruments (while repairs take place) to allow for continuity in musical progress.

## Instrument Trials

Standard industry practice is that musicians of any age or level may take home an instrument free of charge for one week before renting or purchasing. This allows the musician to consult with teachers or peers and to play the instrument in a variety of acoustic settings. **Avoid any shop that does not allow this trial week.** Shops may ask for ID and a credit card number, but charges should not be made unless return of the instrument is delayed or deliberate damage occurs.

## Private Sellers

While many private teachers and professional musicians sell instruments they no longer wish to personally use, buying from a legitimate instrument store protects your investment by providing a location to exchange the instrument when your child is ready for a more advanced one. Additionally, purchasing an instrument from a business rather than an individual provides you with the proper paperwork that would make selling the instrument yourself easier should you ever move away from the shop. Lastly, be aware that sometimes there are little flaws in an instrument that even a professional player would not be able to diagnose. Should one of these flaws result in a broken instrument, it's much easier to pursue a claim with an established business than with a private party.

## Instruments Matter for All Young Musicians

Renting from luthiers and specialist shops is usually not more expensive than renting from all-purpose shops, which often have more visible and expensive storefront locations. Do as much research as you can and check out a few places off the beaten path. Don't be intimidated by music snobs and professional instrument salesmen. The smallest child has the most exciting musical journey still to come, and finding the right instrument is a key part of this fantastic adventure!

## Tone Quality and Playability

High-caliber instruments help kids learn to listen with great sensitivity to the tone quality colors in an instrument's sound. This magical diversity of sound in an instrument can ignite a spark of motivation in a developing musician. Alternatively, a bad instrument can do the opposite. In the worst cases, it causes children to doubt themselves early in the learning process. One luthier put it well to me: "How can a child learn to play and hear different musical tone colors if their instrument only offers shades of black and white? The instrument comes first and artistry develops second."

As they grow up and take music on as part of their identity, young musicians often consider their instrument to be their second voice. Make that voice one that contributes to positive self-esteem. Children who are inspired by the sound of their instruments are more likely to practice on their own and continue playing through difficulties. Those playing instruments that seem to be working against them may refrain from the most difficult practice unless forced. They might find their sound embarrassing and consider it a personal fault. Additionally, it's widely observed among teachers that kids take better care of their instrument when they know it's special.

## *Virtuosity*

High-quality instruments allow for the development of better physical playing technique. Yes, that's right—acquiring a better instrument actually makes playing music easier. The reverse is true as well—poor technique often develops from attempting to compensate for a poor instrument. Advanced instruments truly do give students a fair platform on which to compete, and bad instruments offer an unfair disadvantage. The right instrument aids in the pursuit of virtuosity. An inappropriate instrument hinders musical and technical growth.

Music is, at its core, a phenomenon of physics. Tone quality stems from players' precise physical movements and the physical components of their instruments. To expect great sound from a low-quality instrument is to expect a paper airplane to do the work of a Boeing 747. No matter how talented the child is, they will be held back by an instrument that doesn't support their goals. For example, a higher-quality violin bow will bounce much more easily than a cheap one, making virtuosic techniques like *spiccato* (short, off-the-string notes) easier to acquire.

## The Importance of Sizing

With almost any other investment piece, parents commonly size up to let their child grow into the new item and wear it for longer. With instruments, this is a common but dangerous approach.

An instrument that is too large for its player makes technique more difficult to acquire. Given the extra lesson time your child and their teacher will spend adjusting for bad technique, the wiser financial move is to just buy an appropriately sized instrument. Additionally, advanced repertoire and the corresponding techniques are almost always more difficult on instruments that are too large. To ask a child to perform exceedingly difficult tasks on an instrument and then give them an instrument that directly hinders those tasks is unfair.

Children who play instruments that are too large face more fatigue in lessons and practice than those with correctly sized instruments. Young children may already tire easily when displaying the correct focus in lessons and practice. Adding this physical hindrance puts another obstacle in their path.

Given the prevalence of playing-based injuries, practicing on an oversized instrument is downright risky. Even if a student plays a mid-size instrument for only a few months before moving on to a larger one, it is always worth pursuing an instrument that fits.

Some teachers may prefer children to move up to a larger instrument sooner rather than later, on the theory that it is often less expensive to get better sound through a larger (cheap, low-quality) instrument than it would be to get the same sound through a smaller, better-quality instrument. The physical well-being of the player should never be sacrificed in this pursuit.

## The Danger of Comparisons

As a teacher, I've watched as parents listen to my own playing. Rather than being inspired by the tones and excited for their child's future, some parents cut in with, "That sounds so beautiful!" Then they turn to their child. "Penny, why doesn't it sound like that when you play?! How come you can't make your violin sound like that?"

By comparing their child's playing to the teacher's playing in this way, parents unintentionally imply that the child is the lesser one in the student-teacher team. By contrast, no child is the lesser when compared with their teacher! The child is just at the beginning of their musical journey, and the teacher is much farther along. And, of course, the teacher is likely playing an exceptionally high-quality instrument. Open your children's ears to advanced tone quality by giving them opportunities to hear many fine musicians perform. Let your child aspire to play on that level someday.

Parents often wonder what the secret to professional tone quality is, as if there's a quick-fix a teacher could give. Truthfully, the secret to professional sound is years of training and a solid instrument. There's nothing a teacher can perform that a student would not one day be capable of, given equal training and an equal instrument advantage. **Time, not will or talent, is truly the only missing ingredient.**

## Insurance and Repairs

No matter how careful a child is or how much they love their instrument, accidents happen. Children tend to find these incidents hugely upsetting and most often prefer a repair to getting an entirely new instrument. Either way though, your financial investment will benefit from having appropriate insurance coverage in moments like these. Instrument insurance is relatively inexpensive and easy to obtain.

If your family owns the instrument, it can be added as a specific item (a rider) to your home insurance policy. This is usually the most cost-effective option. Alternatively, several insurance companies specialize in insuring musical instruments.

While most insurance policies won't cover routine maintenance (like new strings, rosin, or bow hair), these policies do come in handy for major repairs from accidental damage. Understand what work on your child's instrument is considered routine maintenance, and therefore comes out of your own pocket, and what repairs are eligible for reimbursement under your insurance policy. The major objective of instrument insurance is to allow unforeseen repairs and replacements to be made immediately, facilitating continued skill development for your child.

# Chapter 8

## Proper Technique and Injury Prevention

*"Raymond says his back hurts when he plays viola. Is that normal?"*

*"Carly says the chin-rest on her violin hurts her jaw. Is this for real, or is she just looking for attention or an excuse not to practice?"*

FEW CHILDREN WILL want to practice daily if their instrument, no matter how beautiful it sounds, causes them physical pain. It's common for students new to my studio to be surprised when I ask them if their shoulders hurt when they play. They smile shyly and admit, "Yes, my shoulders do hurt. How did you know?"

Then we make an agreement: if my students experience any pain that is associated with the instrument, they will tell me, they will tell their parents, and they will tell their orchestra directors. Adults can't fix pain that goes unmentioned!

Why is this so important in music? Children are told in other activities, especially sports, to just suck it up and redouble their efforts when, for example, their legs feel weak. Parents ask why playing instruments is different from sports in this way. "Music isn't even as physical as basketball!" they remark. By contrast, experts—in sports and music—emphasize that too much stress or repetitive activity on any body part can lead to injury.

When families watch professionals perform, the fast musical passages catch everyone's interest. "That must be really difficult!" parents observe. However, while some techniques are tricky, few pieces require brute physical strength on string instruments. Advanced pieces can be safely learned if children are taught to pay attention to any discomfort and to always bring these issues to the attention of teachers. Indeed, true virtuosity on instruments comes from relaxed and healthy muscle memory as well as the accuracy that proper technique facilitates.

---

### Asymmetrical Postures and Repetitive Movements

Most musical instruments inherently involve asymmetrical posture and repetitive movements. Left unchecked over years of daily practice (often for hours on end—especially in orchestra rehearsals), these conditions can lead to injuries. Excessive tension or exhaustion exacerbates this process. While we can't go back in time and redesign the violin or cello for different ergonomics, we can modify the way we approach practicing, posture, and performance to keep musicians' bodies happy and healthy.

---

## Tension

Counterintuitively, tension is actually the enemy of control, and its presence foretells a heightened struggle with accuracy, speed, and musicality. In the early stages of learning a new instrument, everyone experiences tension. For example, when one focuses intensely on a task, brows furrow and muscles tense, reflecting heightened concentration and effort. In studying music, the first battle students face is learning how to play without that tension.

To help parents identify with this struggle over tension and technique, many teachers ask parents to practice on full-size instruments through the first few months of a child's study. This is a brilliant strategy because it allows parents to experience the early (and significant) technical challenges on the instrument, providing an invaluable window into the learning process. And, even better, it shows children that the skills they are developing on the instrument aren't easily acquired. Persistence and great attention to detail are required from everyone—even grownups!

When parents first join my studio, they tell me they can't believe how nuanced and sophisticated the movements I ask their children to demonstrate are. Parents admit they're just plain overwhelmed or daunted by this complexity, even as adults. "That's okay," I tell them. "Playing an instrument is more complicated than anyone realizes when they first set out. The great news is that you are about to see a whole new capability in your child—soon to far surpass your own!"

## The Violin Vortex & Strategically Scheduled Breaks

When young musicians are practicing, breaks may feel inefficient. Who wants to deliberately carve out extra practice time for breaks when there's an important audition coming up? Still, both focus and physical ability falter when students practice for overextended stretches. Teach your child to recognize when they feel foggy. If they find themselves attempting the same technique several times in a row without achieving positive and sustainable results, they have fallen into a Violin Vortex.

A Violin Vortex means a player has lost their mental focus. In frustration, they just attempt the same thing over and over, faster each time. This rushing builds physical tension and leads to sloppier results (instead of more precise ones), provoking even more frustration! Listen carefully for the Violin Vortex phenomenon during your child's practice. When you hear it, show your child how to take healthy breaks from intense effort to keep work productive.

Breaks ensure proper technical development because putting the instrument down and picking it up again is a chance to check posture and positioning, taking stock of what might have slipped. These checks are absolutely essential for minimizing bad habits and tension. Even for advanced musicians who have long solidified their correct playing posture, taking timely and appropriate breaks relieves any muscle tension and enables fresh focus.

There's a huge difference between playing for five hours straight and playing five sessions of forty-five minutes each, separated by scheduled fifteen-minute breaks: the former will take a far greater physical toll on any musician, regardless of age. In this sense, to truly participate in effective practicing, young musicians need to allow extra time when planning practice sessions. For example, if a violinist has two hours' worth of work to do in the practice room, the schedule for that day should allow for two and a half to three hours of practice time. Help your child understand this relationship between the amount of time they wish to spend working on notes each day and the amount of time they actually need to schedule (to account for breaks).

## Standing Well

Determined young musicians sometimes lock their knees and take only shallow breaths as they concentrate in lesson or during practice at home. The unfortunate side effect of this is that they begin to feel dizzy, sometimes to the point of fainting. Even if this is not an issue at home or in lessons, it pops up occasionally in performances when young musicians are too preoccupied with nerves to notice their posture. Coaching young musicians to develop great posture habits (with knees relaxed) is crucial for safety and will pay off with improved stamina and resilience during performances as well.

## Stay Hydrated

It's difficult to stay alert when one is dehydrated, and musicians' bodies need water to facilitate efficient physical movement on instruments. At the end of a long school day, many of my students come to lesson and realize they're thirsty—they haven't been able to drink much water all day. Through long rehearsals, lessons, and practice sessions, it's important for your child to have easy access to water. Help your child develop the habit of carrying a water bottle with them to rehearsals. This comes back to the old rule that musicians (especially children!) who feel well, play well.

## Always Warm Up

Performers on all instruments benefit from two types of warm-ups. First, players should ensure their hands (or, for singers, their voices) are physically warm before practicing, especially if the selected repertoire is technically demanding. Playing with cold hands predisposes musicians to injury. Running hands briefly under warm water makes a huge difference in accuracy and agility on string instruments. One wouldn't sprint a mile without warming up, and sprinting on the cello and violin is no different. If it's extremely cold outside, musicians should wear mittens, which keep fingers warmer than gloves do, before coming inside to practice. Similarly, many professionals swear by hand-warmers at auditions. Overzealous air conditioning leaves audition rooms cold, and young musicians benefit immensely from having a way to keep their hands warm until they are ready to perform.

The second type of warm-up is on the instrument itself. By starting practice with familiar, consistent repertoire, musicians can check and reconfirm their technique. For example, a habit of starting each session by playing scales with good wrist posture makes it far easier for a violinist to maintain that same posture through difficult pieces. A word of caution: many young musicians, focused on their musical to-do list, skip scale warm-ups. Teachers can always tell in lessons when this has happened because the overall technique for that week will have suffered.

## Every Day Counts

"Lauren, did you practice today? You know, every day you either get better or worse, but you don't stay the same!" I heard those words all the time growing up. My parents were eager to remind me that it's impossible to stay the same level day to day as a musician. Thanks to muscle and sensory memory, a musician's skill level either improves or drops with each passing day.

The more time between practice sessions, the more a musician will tend to use tension to make up for accuracy lost during the time off. If, for example, a child practices every other day for an hour, they will likely play their instrument with considerably more physical tension than a child who practices every day for thirty minutes. The same amount of weekly time is spent on the instrument, but the results will be drastically different. Additionally, the child practicing daily will find that practice time passes more quickly and is more productive because they spend less time trying to remember what they were working on forty-eight hours before. To really maximize this benefit, teach your child that even on a day when they may not be able to commit to a full practice session, taking the instrument out of the case and playing a few scales will go far in preventing muscle memory loss.

Some gaps between practice sessions cannot be avoided. Extended family vacations, for example, can cause trouble in this way. Don't encourage your child to go from missing a week of playing to suddenly practicing for five hours a day—that's a recipe for tension. Plan for this adjustment before you leave town and gradually build back to your child's regular routine after you have returned.

## Red Flags for Tension

How can you know when your child is really hurting versus when they're just using it as an excuse to get out of practicing? Bring their teacher in on all discussions related to pain and the instrument. The first thing their teacher will do is make sure that the instrument is appropriately sized and is in good, playable condition. Accessories like shoulder rests, chin rests (for violins and violas), and endpins (for cellos) should be properly fitted as well. Then your child's teacher should carefully observe—is the painful area a spot where your child has been holding tension as they play?

For example, in overcrowded orchestra programs, students may be crammed together to fit into a too-small rehearsal space. As such, students can let their positioning warp: slouching and similar "space-saving" bad habits develop. Ask your child's teacher to model how one should share a stand with another musician in orchestra rehearsals.

For new string players, fingertips may be a little sore in the beginning—calluses will soon develop and the issue will resolve itself. Students learning other instruments may develop healthy and normal physical adaptations like this as well. But it's *always* worth checking with teachers on what your child should or should not be feeling when they practice. Another common source of trouble is the height of a child's music stand at home. If the stand is too low or too high for a musician to comfortably view, back or other pain may result.

Be conscious of whether your child stands or sits in lessons versus while practicing at home. If they stand in lesson, but then sit at home to practice, this provides an opportunity for developing poor posture that their teacher would not be able to recognize and correct. Keep in mind that seated instruments (cello, for example) require an instrument-specific chair at home. As a bonus, these chairs encourage good posture. Avoid having your child practice in any chair that has arm rests or makes healthy playing posture challenging.

## Fixing Bad Technique

When intermediate students initially join advanced music studios, their new teachers find significant opportunity to improve technique. Often, students will have developed less than ideal habits while playing in a school orchestra (especially if they did not previously have the benefit of private lessons). Orchestra directors are amazing people, but it's nearly impossible to convey every physical nuance to a room full of young musicians on various instruments. Sometimes, students join new studios following years of study with a private teacher whose own technique training was poor.

However, the older a musician is and the longer they've played, the more challenging it is to make major technique changes. This phenomenon makes it incredibly frustrating for children when teachers modify unhealthy playing techniques that for years went uncorrected. The concepts are often so simple—"Relax your thumb!"—that players become angry at themselves, wrestling with the reality of how difficult it is to modify subtle yet ingrained muscle memory habits.

The conversion from tension-based playing to consciously relaxed (and advanced) instrumental technique requires persistence. Students must re-identify and then fix the same issue dozens and dozens of times over the course of weeks (sometimes even months!) to truly banish these old habits, while the old ghost—muscle memory—tries to creep back in.

When a challenge like this arises for a child, parents are usually surprised. They had no idea that, for example, their child's last teacher might have neglected these playing aspects or that closer parental supervision during practice might have prevented such issues. Take heart: it's okay to experience this difficult stage because the persistence required to develop functional technique is one of the soft skills quality musical education teaches.

The secret to building new technique and erasing old bad habits is frequent reinforcement and teamwork, with reminders ("How's your thumb?") from parents during practice and the teacher in lessons. For players who are old enough to practice effectively alone, playing in front of a mirror prompts posture awareness and prevents undesirable habits from sneaking into the middle of a familiar etude. Mirrors allow musicians to constantly evaluate their physical motions as they play—complex, nuanced movements are difficult to perceive correctly without the added visual assistance.

Here's one way to ensure frequent reinforcement of new techniques whilst developing self-direction in your child. Have them practice their instrument in front of a mirror. Every time their hands try to form the old habit while they work, have them stop, fix their positioning, and put a penny in an empty mug. The entire mug should be full of pennies by the following lesson if they have been correcting their old habit consistently enough.

Parents, you can provide crucial feedback through this intense "technique makeover" process. Because young musicians often can't physically feel the difference when their technique has lapsed, you (with your external and objective visual advantage) can alert your child (perhaps by putting pennies in the jar yourself) whenever you see their posture or technique shift back to the old habits. There is no skipping over this process of helpful repetition, so reward it by offering enthusiasm and encouragement.

# Part 3
# Build Resilience
# and Maturity

# Chapter 9

# Competitions: Preparing for Peak Performance

*"How is it possible that Kate didn't win this one? She was the most advanced player by far! What do we need to do to win?"*

AUDITION WINS AND losses are powerful motivators and can tremendously influence future musical and academic opportunities. From school chair tests to scholarship competitions and conservatory auditions, it's crucial for your child to understand how to represent their highest level of playing at every performance. In this chapter, learn how to help them prepare musically, mentally, and physically before performances. Take an in-depth look at subjectivity and learn how to talk about it with your family. Establish your child's brand as a performer by fostering stage presence and leadership. Most importantly, learn how your family can build on wins and bounce back from losses.

## Physical and Mental Competition Preparation

The first thing to know about audition preparation is that young musicians' performance levels are subject to tremendous variance depending on three things: adequate preparation on the musical material, mental state, and physical comfort. These three factors either work for or against your child in terms of tone quality, memory, vibrato, intonation, and musicality. For example, a child who plays spectacularly well on a Friday night may still perform poorly the following day (representing a truly different level of proficiency) if their day-of preparation is off somehow. By teaching your child how to control these three factors (adequate musical preparation, a productive mental state, and physical comfort), you can help them achieve peak mental and physical performance when it counts.

Like many teachers, I have my students read aloud positive affirmations (on notecards) in the weeks leading up to auditions. My students laugh and blush the first time they read these confidence-inspiring statements about themselves, but by the last lesson before their performance, focus and confidence have taken root. The flash cards have real power to change a young musician's mindset—daily affirmations bring assurance that each performance will be successful.

Next, recognize that all competition performances, no matter how mentally difficult, hinge on physical wellness. Children may feel queasy the morning of a big audition, but it's essential that they eat protein. Skipping breakfast can lead to dizziness, fainting, or foggy thinking later in the day. Given that many school-sponsored competitions take up an entire Saturday, it's crucial that the competitors have had enough protein, rather than sugar, prior to arriving. For string players, packing a snack that doesn't leave fingers sticky is also important. Young musicians should also remember to drink water at events to stay energized and focused.

Quality sleep, too, helps musicians stay sharp through long audition days. Advise your child to always choose an appropriate amount of sleep (the night before an audition) over last-minute preparation. All-nighters frazzle nerves and delay reaction times. To maximize your child's focus and energy, follow this strategy: if a competition starts early in the morning, have your child wake up early for the full week before the competition. For example, if they need to be at peak musical performance at 8 a.m. on a Saturday, they might strategically wake up at 6 a.m. each day for the prior week.

An essential component of musical performance is the precise movements of small muscles. The accuracy of these movements first thing in the morning is enhanced greatly by having students shower the morning of a competition. Doing so wakes up their muscles and gets circulation moving. This step is especially crucial for string players, as it displaces any swelling of the fingers that happens overnight. Many parents advise children to shower the night before a competition (to save a few minutes of sleep the morning of), but this is actually counterproductive. Instead, students will simply feel more energized when the burst of water in the shower hits them.

Strategic competition preparation in coordination with a child's routine provides immense reassurance and comfort, even to older players. By contrast, experiencing a drastically different day than usual—waking up at 5 a.m. rather than 8 a.m., skipping a shower and breakfast, and driving somewhere unfamiliar—can throw performers for a loop. In preparation for events, retain as much of your normal routine as possible (for example, if everyone always has breakfast together, do that). If possible, set your child's expectations by visiting the venue the week before.

Now that we know how big a role physical comfort plays in performance situations, let's strategize how to take care of a performer's comfort at an audition as well. Audition rooms are often either very hot or cold. For example, the temperature in a room of two hundred violinists can be impossible to control well on a Saturday when the building's maintenance staff is away. Similarly, stage lights can make performers uncomfortably warm, but large halls can grow quite cold without a full audience. Given the importance of temperature in any musician's ability to produce good tone quality, additional preparation before the competition is prudent. Instruments also suffer when a room is too cold or hot—ask your child's teacher how your child might deal with this as it relates to their specific instrument.

If it's too warm, string players complain of sweaty fingers. Too cold, and they can't seem to get their fingers to move fast or accurately enough. Similarly, wind and brass players complain that the room temperature throws their instruments out of tune too frequently. Address concerns like this by advising performers to dress in layers, bring hand-warmers (even in summer competitions to combat frigid air conditioning), and pack a cloth to wipe away sweat that appears on the fingerboard. As parents and teachers, we may not be able to control venue temperature, but we can take small steps to ensure comfort.

Remember that playing with cold hands is physically unhealthy for string players. Musicians are more likely to injure themselves when they "play cold." Prevent this by having your child warm up at home (by practicing) prior to driving to the venue, dress in layers, bring the aforementioned hand-warmers, and do a few arm circles (or other exercises as advised by their teacher) before performing.

---

### Choose Competitions and Repertoire Wisely

Competitions develop both motivation and talent in young musicians in that these events prompt intense musical effort and growth. With your child's teacher, identify local competitions that involve the appropriate level of repertoire. Signing up for a competition that calls for inappropriately advanced repertoire is like trying to build a house with just a hammer and nails. Sure, you could do it, but it's not the best use of your effort (or your child's). Between competitions, build your child's "musical toolbox" so they have everything they need to pursue future competition repertoire.

---

## Pre-Competition Talks

When you try to prepare your child in case the competition results bring disappointment, you hear yourself protecting their self-esteem. They hear you acknowledging (and possibly validating) their fear that they are not good enough (to their ears: a loser). This is the gap between parental intention and parental impact. Instead, simply acknowledge that, as a rule, competition results are never the last word on talent or potential. Preparing for a competition provides the opportunity to grow musically, and properly analyzing the results (favorable or not) is a chance to reflect on how to compete more effectively in the future. The lessons and strategies learned through challenging experiences represent didactic trophies as young musicians grow. These difficulties are merely investments in the development of your child's strength.

Parents tell me that they avoid reassuring their child before a competition because they fear that doing so would put too much pressure on their child, heightening competition expectations. By contrast, when a child has worked hard these affirmations from others give budding confidence some much-needed substantiation! Teach your child to believe these reassurances by accepting compliments from others yourself.

In your pre-competition talks with your child, affirm your unconditional love and respect: "I love you. We will do this competition together for your musical and emotional growth." Too often teachers hear parents say, "I love you, even if you lose on Sunday!" In response to statements like this, young musicians blush and look down at their toes, already imagining a loss. Instead, remove winning or losing from the dialogue completely. *Of course* everyone wants to win. *Of course* you will love your child no matter what!

Cheerleaders cheer every game as if it's the season's best, even when they know their team might lose. Create similar excitement for each competition by curating pre-performance conversations to build resilience without references to potential competition results.

---

### Manage Expectations and Review Past Performances

Your child's teacher should be familiar with the history and standards of the musical competitions your child wishes to pursue. Likewise, consider asking the parents of former competitors in these specific events for their advice. Your child, too, can be a source of competition advice: have them write short journal entries after each competition to provide lessons learned for future performances.

---

## Focus the Nerves Away: Moves Not Grooves

One of my studio's favorite mantras before competitions is Moves Not Grooves. Moves Not Grooves reminds competitors that they retain more power over their focus and performance when they purposely bring their attention to specific finger movements (Moves) instead of letting their mind wander by default to their current feelings (Grooves) about the audition. Students realize that by choosing to notice their physical actions, there is less room for nerves to take over during performances.

In the beginning, focusing on finger movements takes effort—it's so easy to slip into frenzied anxiety on stage. Teachers and parents can help performers adjust to this thought pattern by encouraging children (during practice) to focus on their finger movements instead of on the upcoming competition. I find that when students make clumsy mistakes in lessons, it's because their mind has wandered to their upcoming performance. I always ask, "Sean, are you thinking, 'If I play it just like this on Saturday, will I get in to the orchestra?'"

My students always answer that yes, that's exactly what they were thinking at the moment of their clumsiness. Whenever students practice while thinking of an upcoming competition, they are not really practicing their notes—they're practicing being distracted by anxiety! Of course, when students rehearse their anxiety like this along with their playing, that anxiety will show up in a big way on competition day. Instead, take note of everyone's tendency to do this and instruct your child to practice drawing their focus back to their fingers and musicality.

Some educators tell young musicians to, "Imagine this is the performance right now, as you play through your piece!" during rehearsals. This strategy is counterproductive: it creates a habit of excessive distraction. When children do this, they merely practice the art of performing on autopilot while totally distracted by anxiety. They really are "somewhere else" as they play. If musicians play while focusing on anticipated concert emotions (usually anxiety) instead of focusing on finger movements, the performance will be based on emotions and distracted thinking instead of the physical movements that performers need to remember. Instead of training to remember a B-flat each time they play measure 249, they train to be in Anxiety Land at measure 249. A more productive approach is to tell your child that they can imagine the competition when they are away from the instrument. Better yet, visit the performance venue together to understand what to expect.

To further substantiate this, consider the mindset of top surgeons. It's commonly said that when surgeons perform operations, they are hammers that see only nails. In this way, surgeons avoid humanizing the patient they work on. Surgery is so nuanced that surgeons—even ones performing life-saving operations—must focus only on the task at hand. They firmly shut the door to any anxiety over whether a patient might live or die. Surgeons do not distract themselves by questioning possible outcomes in the middle of surgery. To do so would put their patient in danger because of the high focus levels surgery requires. Young musicians need to follow the same strategy. Tell your child to focus on the notes. In the middle of a performance, nothing else matters. Retaining control over onstage focus is a sign of musical maturity.

Everyone admires the player whose performance seems enhanced and emboldened by the presence of an audience. While parents often attribute this phenomenon to a natural talent for the spotlight, this ability can be developed in anyone. Musicians whose focus is only intensified by the scrutiny of an audience are created, not born. The secret to developing this strength is to perform well-mastered pieces for welcoming audiences as often as possible.

---

### Play Until the Whistle Blows

Teach your child to keep playing no matter what happens in a performance. Liken competition performances to sports, in which the game isn't over until the whistle blows to officially end the match. Children should learn to focus on each new note as they play it, rather than let their focus slip to any previous note they perceive has just hurt their chances. The objective is to give the best possible performance through to the last note.

---

## A Note on Speed

We're all familiar with that one older, scary-looking violinist warming up with full-speed Paganini while the rest of the violinists in the room stumble, distracted, through the competition's actual repertoire. Usually, the show-off competitor in the room is just nervous and their fast playing is an outlet for their extra energy. Sometimes they have been told by a teacher to play loudly and with great speed to intimidate other competitors.

Often, this unsportsmanlike behavior works—other young musicians in the room panic, feeling inferior. As a result, they begin running through musical passages in "nerve mode," busy experiencing an adrenaline rush instead of thinking about their notes. In doing so, they undo the physical accuracy that had been drilled into their playing slowly over weeks of practice.

Performance results are highly correlated with muscle memory. Unfortunately, the physical effect of nerves often throws these precise physical movements out of position. Additionally, because muscles have been hard-wired to be efficient, muscles frequently try to find ways to "cheat" to facilitate speed. For example, speed might make the pinky less inclined to reach all the way up to a C# on the violin, and instead the finger lands just short of the C# before dashing back down the fingerboard to reach another note. Teachers commonly observe that when students practice a piece daily with the tempo as written (full speed), this efficient, rather than accurate, move becomes the norm. In the days before a competition—and especially the day of—it is crucial to bring the performance piece back down in tempo to ensure accuracy.

Prior to recitals and competitions, my colleagues and I catch our students—who certainly know better!—giving in to nerves and performing their pieces fast in the practice rooms, just to prove to themselves that they can do it. In doing so, students stress themselves out and set themselves up for a more emotion-based (rather than a mindful movement-based) performance. In response to this widespread tendency, many teachers go so far as to ban students from playing anything up to speed within twenty-four hours of an event—the first full-speed run-through on the day is the competition performance itself. Through this rule, slow and accurate repetition in practice ensures that fingers stay accurate and that adrenaline isn't triggered too soon.

Help your child resist adrenaline-based speed traps. Provide a calm atmosphere the morning of performances, and remind your child to practice slowly and focus on small groups of notes. After a few auditions, your family will have these strategies down to a science!

## Help Your Child Understand Their Brand

As your child seeks leadership opportunities in orchestras and bands, consider that all young musicians have a personal brand, or reputation. If a child's school-year brand is that they are consistently disruptive or unprepared in rehearsals, even an incredible audition at the end of the year won't lead to a leadership desk or placement in a more advanced orchestra. Past behavior, a key element of any child's personal brand, is inextricably included in the judges' holistic evaluation of the child's ability to contribute to the orchestra. It's not enough to just be a fabulous player: to be an ensemble's concertmaster (or another principal player), leadership and maturity are essential traits. This is something orchestra directors commonly tell parents and private teachers.

Some of the most important signals children send are the ones they send unintentionally. When, after a disappointing chair test, a child slouches back in their orchestra seat with a scowl, they fail to demonstrate the maturity and resilience required to advance to a high-rank chair. The child is perceived as acting out their hurt feelings: they appear to have a wounded sense of entitlement. By contrast, a child ready to advance demonstrates musical sportsmanship, trying their best each rehearsal regardless of competition or chair test results.

## Leaders Show Kindness

Another way for musicians to demonstrate their leadership talent is through genuine kindness to younger players. I see this amongst my students and encourage it at every opportunity. One of the most obvious features of world-class musicians is their graciousness. For example, Itzhak Perlman and Yo-Yo Ma are known for their warmth toward absolutely every musician—professionals, students, and amateurs alike—they meet.

Teachers and youth orchestra directors notice that young musicians who are just below the top level in an ensemble—the ones desperately trying to break through and stand out—sometimes demonstrate the opposite behavior. Aggressive, bullying behavior is evident in other classes outside of music too, and is too often dismissed as "just how things are in school."

In competitive youth orchestras, it can feel like every player in a leadership role has a knife in their back from someone at the back of the orchestra. Teach your child to keep their eyes on the prize—musical collaboration and excellence—and to not engage in negative behavior. They should strongly reject that behavior from others and not let rivalries or disappointments influence their own behavior.

When your child is associated with kindness and preparedness, their positive brand as a musician will pay off in bringing them greater leadership opportunities, both musical and otherwise.

## Stage Presence

Stage presence includes posture, facial expressions, and basic performance etiquette. Because many judges don't realize how much competitors' appearances affect judges' perceptions of playing ability, stage presence is absolutely crucial in any competition. A common reminder for young performers is that audiences "listen with their eyes" as well as with their ears.

Work with your child to develop stage posture (standing or sitting tall). Remind them to avoid any winces or scowls during a performance, regardless of the sounds being produced. Many times, these facial expressions are the most salient clues that a note was supposed to have sounded better.

Musicians find that rehearsing scripted stage presence movements—everything from how to walk on stage, how to bow, and how to cue their accompanist to begin the performance—prepares them to be calmer and more confident on stage. A solid performance routine like this facilitates easier focus and, as a bonus, makes a stronger impression on the audience. Consider the visual of how professionals bow (confidently, facing the audience) versus the way beginning players bow (only a bob of the head, if at all, and often not entirely facing the audience). What a difference it makes when a performer, through a proper bow, acknowledges the audience!

## Dress

Appearances matter—it's not shallow to teach your kids that presentation, in addition to the music itself, is important. Children are often incredibly sensitive about their appearance, so the topic can be difficult to broach. As any parent knows, comments on appearance, no matter how well-intended, can backfire, so it's worth considering carefully how to proceed.

Recognize that well-chosen, well-fitting, and appropriate attire is an inescapable part of the competition requirements. Put time on your side—decide with your child when you sign up for the competition what their dress and grooming on competition day will be. Make such decisions routine by sticking with a proven performance uniform your child likes, and update its elements as they grow.

Listen without judgment when your child tells you that part of their outfit causes discomfort. For example, the physical movements required to perform on many instruments are genuinely more difficult in a suit with shoulder pads, buttons, or ornaments. Have full dress rehearsals ahead of time to iron out any of these kinks. Always scuff the bottoms of new shoes (especially heels) to make them less slippery on shiny stage floors. By giving your child an appropriate "costume routine," you show them how taking control of their wardrobe builds confidence before performances. With these details under control in advance, your young musician can feel confident on stage and focus on their instrument instead of on appearance-based insecurities.

### Pursue Tone Quality Advantages

This inherent lack of control for variables in competitions means you are free to pursue advantages for your child. On the simple side, consult with your child's teacher to ensure their instrument will be in top shape for the competition. Make sure each part of their instrument is clean and well-maintained. For example, replace old strings, bow hair, and rosin according to your teacher's prescribed timeline. These relatively inexpensive adjustments can provide a huge tone quality payoff and therefore give your child an edge over other competitors.

## Understand Subjectivity

There are times to point out injustices and unfairness, and there are times when we have to realize that we can't change this machine—instead, we have to learn how to work it. This skill (balancing respect for the way the world turns with an eye for inappropriate situations) will keep your child's self-esteem afloat as they navigate the workforce as an adult someday. Point out to your child that we cannot control judging accuracy, we can only control our own preparation and resilience.

When young musicians and their parents aren't able to understand subjectivity, they perceive it as bias or unfairness (blaming the world) or as a weakness on their part (blaming themselves). Blaming the world gives children a reason to be angry or stop trying their best. Blaming themselves paralyzes future efforts, creating a feeling of hopelessness.

Children don't have the maturity to understand subjectivity. As adults, sometimes we too fall short in understanding this phenomenon. However, we can seize moments like competitions to explain subjectivity. As a parent, your job is not to rage against a loss, but to communicate these difficulties to your child in a way that never causes them to question their self-worth or lose faith in the system.

For example, a father in my studio was shocked to learn that the "blind"' auditions (where judges rank players only through hearing, rather than seeing, them) that his children were doing for chair tests in their youth orchestra were not actually blind. The judges could indeed see the musicians from their vantage point and had seemingly arranged players according to age and other factors (instead of according to actual performance levels). Another ensemble parent, upon discovering this, chose to withdraw her son from that orchestra for the following year. While we can all see the unfairness in auditions like this, withdrawing from activities in reaction does far more harm than good. Removing a child from participation provides them with an escape from the world instead of a view into it. Even unfair or misleading competitions provide you with the chance to grow closer to your child when discussing the matter together.

## Challenging the Results

Obvious favoritism from a judge, poor enforcement of competition rules, even interruptions from the audience in the middle of a child's performance—the frequency of these misfortunes doesn't make them any less infuriating. While we should always strive for the best and expect fairness, it doesn't always happen.

When unfairness strikes, the emotion is understandable. You're furious. Your child poured hours of their best work into their preparation. You couldn't be prouder of them. You see the injustice and you want things to be right. You want to have some impact. You're tempted to quit the orchestra, drop out of the competition. You're tempted to make a fuss, call out the adjudicators, speak with the coach, fire the teachers. Doing so, however, never results in any adjustment in the results. It only undermines both you and your child.

Consider these three paths before you and your child. The first path is anger at the system for perceived injustices. The second is frustration directed toward yourself or your child for perceived flaws ("Why did you forget measure twenty-three? I should have taken you to that extra lesson!"). By contrast, the third path is merely increased resilience. This third option develops maturity. Disappointment may tempt you to veer toward the first two paths and unintentionally demonstrate anger and frustration in front of your child, but we can work together to choose this third path instead.

Understand that competitions are fundamentally unable to publicly acknowledge subjectivity or weak spots—doing so would invalidate these events. For the sake of the public, everyone needs to have faith in these competitions. Subjectivity is real, but institutions can't acknowledge it too much and still stand by these events and their results. Since there is no true way to fully remove subjectivity, show your child how to deal with these setbacks as they mature.

You don't want to cause lasting political damage to your child's brand by fighting the results. Do you want your child to be remembered in this competition as the well-prepared kid who just didn't win this time around, or do you want them to be thought of as the kid with the hot-headed parent? Any parental protest over results will overshadow a child's effort far more than the actual loss.

Whenever a young musician applies for a scholarship, competition, performance, or orchestra, they interact with people in the music industry. If your child is thinking of entering the music field, they will run into the same people again and again throughout their career. Avoid burning bridges or doing anything that might embarrass them. Instead, think of each competition as a political deposit—thanks to each new event, your child's name becomes known to more people. Your child may not win, but they've got their foot in the door with these connections in the future.

## Remember Your Purpose

Is the goal of winning an event one step further along the path to an even greater accomplishment? If a child's goal is to become an elite musician, both wins and losses are part of that path. A loss does not call for a referendum on the feasibility of future musical endeavors.

What is the purpose of pursuing these competitions? All those hours of competition-specific repertoire preparation imply that the ultimate goal is to win. However, competition results may fail to reflect the intense growth children experience when they prepare for and carry out their audition. Due to innate subjectivity (or to competing against musicians who are further along in their musical education), a child's effort isn't always recognized in terms of prizes as much or as soon as they might like it to be.

Remember that the early stages of any learning process are inevitably more difficult than they would appear to be at first. If your child is not winning yet, it's because they have more learning to do. That's okay—developing into a performer is a process, and this is just one part of it.

**Wins and Losses are Variables. Self-confidence is the Constant.**

Sometimes competitors and their families feel it's preferable to be invisible than to be visibly mediocre. When parents believe it's better to not participate in a competition than to publicly suffer a loss, a growth opportunity is wasted. Despite the variables we can't control in competitions, our prerogative as teachers and parents is to show young musicians that goals and competitions are absolutely worth every ounce of effort. Protect your child from the narrative that says because art and music competitions cannot be one-hundred percent objective, these competitions aren't worth pursuing.

With each competition, instrumentalists have an opportunity to grow and further realize their potential. On the flip side, each competition also brings the opportunity to learn negative thinking. True, sometimes judges' comments sting and sometimes results are inaccurate. Occasionally, a child perceives that they've been "robbed"—the competition prize that should have gone to them went to another player instead. In these tough moments, inspire growth, honesty, and persistence in your child. Seize the opportunity to repeat healthy phrases on the value of their own work and persistence. Have your child repeat this mantra:

*"I'm sticking with this musical work because I believe in myself. No struggle will force me to give up. I'm building my own musical future."*

No matter how skilled your child is, the world practically guarantees that tough losses will happen. Embrace the growth opportunities these moments provide. Both victories and losses have immense power to positively impact your child's overall development.

It's heartbreaking to see talented young musicians question their potential because of (in some cases almost arbitrary) competition results. Competitions are meant to spur improvement and inspire self-direction. However, in experiencing unfavorable results or bad governing from teachers and judges, young musicians sometimes perceive this message: "Don't try. You're not talented enough. The word of the judges is the end-all, be-all."

Too often, when children (especially busy teenagers) audition poorly, it's obvious to teachers that *the child didn't believe in their own potential* enough to even justify the investment of their time. In this way, children sometimes don't put forth their best effort because they don't want to feel foolish in front of friends and family. However, even through difficulties like these, you as a parent can provide moments of clarity, introspection, and honesty.

## Take the Negativity Out of Disappointment

Disappointment is not the demon it's made out to be. It can spur motivation and self-reflection, building resilience and maturity. Let your child be upset initially, let them analyze the loss, and then remind them that it doesn't define them.

The more you fear disappointment for your child and teach them to fear it too, the more you imply that competition results validate musical potential. This narrative is dangerous. The complex variables (ranging from subjectivity to competing against a child with a vastly superior instrument) involved in competitions that place subjective rewards on some children over others mean that no competition could ever be a finite evaluation of a young child's worth, talent, merit, or potential.

Yet, some parents take these competition results as a sign of whether their child should continue to pursue an instrument. Want a guarantee that your child will not grow up to be talented? Let them quit. Otherwise, stay on track and use competitions (favorable results or not) to teach your child that talent will come from ever-persistent effort. Do you want to teach your child that the world's evaluations will determine their merit or happiness with themselves, or do you want to teach them that the world is theirs if they just keep pushing despite setbacks?

As an adult, you remember the losses you experienced as a child. Waiting for your name to be called, willingly settling for any space on the team, your heart sunk with every name on the list that wasn't yours. Instead of feeling special or chosen, you felt alienated. Losses seemed to validate your insecurities; watching your child experience the same feeling is crushing. You think to yourself that this isn't why your family invests in music.

One of the most annoying reassurances after a loss is that, "Someday, you will be glad this happened, because things will turn out for the best." However, as unsatisfying as this refrain is, it's true. Sure, young musicians would always prefer the convenience of winning now, receiving public validation of their talent and dreams. Still, at the end of the day, losses strengthen musicians in more powerful ways than wins do, and they guide the path to lifelong excellence. Happiness should not be determined by the results of any one competition. The right accolades and experiences will come into your child's life as they grow.

# Chapter 10

## Fear-Free Creativity

*"My wife is an accountant, and I manage a restaurant. I'm not sure how James is going to do in music and the arts, because the creativity gene definitely won't come from us!"*

AS A TEACHER, I can't tell you how often I hear parents worry that, because they're not artists, their child might struggle. Take heart in understanding that skills like musical talent and artistic creativity are not born—they are developed. Every child—and every person, no matter the age!—can excel in the arts.

The first step to developing fear-free creativity in your child is to show them that creative impulses aren't just for artists. Engineers are creative when they build new machines and projects. Managers are creative when they balance complex business goals with an understanding of what drives the people around them. Mathematicians are creative in applying complex rules to solve problems. In every field, daily work generates opportunities and issues: people generate solutions. By sharing how you use your own creativity daily, you show your child how pursue it as well. You encourage free thinking and self-motivation.

## Just Say, "Okay!"

It's true: children have the most ridiculous ideas sometimes. It's easy to dismiss these daydreams, especially given that children tend to be so unaware of real-world constrictions. By contrast, one way to foster brave creativity in your child is to just ask, "Why not?" and play along with their idea. When you do this, you teach your child that their thoughts are worth sharing. Even as an adult, do you ever hesitate to mention an idea to someone, for fear of looking foolish? When you treat even the silliest ideas like magical creative sparks, you welcome bravery in the sharing of ideas, hopes, and dreams.

To illustrate this, let me tell you a story. When I was little, my father worked as an engineer. He prided himself on finding solutions to every possible problem—silly or practical. My mother sometimes called his solutions to household maintenance issues Home Deprovements, instead of Home Improvements, because his ideas didn't always work out as planned. Still, when they did, it was glorious. One fall, I told my father I would love nothing more than to be a flowerpot for Halloween. Some parents might have ignored my idea, or at least brought up a more conventional alternative. Had this happened when I told my father my idea for a flowerpot costume, I might have inferred from that interaction that my costume idea was ridiculous, and that perhaps my creativity was just silly or worthless in general.

Instead, my father said, "Okay!" We went to the store where all creative fathers take their creative daughters—Home Depot. My dad helped me cut huge cardboard boxes into a gigantic flowerpot shape that I could wear over my clothes on Halloween—it was a bit like cardboard overalls, to be honest. I colored in the huge cardboard flowers in crayon. Totally unafraid of looking ridiculous compared with the other trick-or-treaters, I went all in with fear-free creativity. For about $15, I felt like I had the best Halloween idea and costume ever—along with the best father, too.

## Finding Creative Mentors

In your circle of friends and acquaintances, seek out mentors who notice and bring attention to your child's effort. Effort is truly a catalyst for progress, and if a teacher doesn't highlight and encourage it, students have a much harder time achieving new tasks. Creative mentors see a project in its early stages and see hope. Those who haven't developed this understanding see a project in its early stages and discard it: they are unable to look past this initial "beginner phase" to see potential for growth.

In the business world, companies invest in thought leaders—people whose groundbreaking ideas will shape the future and bring positive disruption to the workplace. Successful companies encourage creativity and create an atmosphere (exemplified by many start-ups in Silicon Valley) in which every idea is worthy of consideration. Think of your child's teachers as your family's personal board of thought leaders and academic directors—who's in charge of math? Who's in charge of English? As you name each mentor to your child's educational board, consider which ones might be able to guide you through encouraging creativity in both academics and music. Some parents might find there's a gap here—in teaching to specific school and state tests, there's not always an official place for creativity in a child's academic environment. This is where private mentors, like music teachers, can work well with your family.

## It's Glam Black

For one of my first professional engagements in London as a violinist and violist, I was playing in the prestigious Queen Elizabeth Hall with the Wally Fields Jazz Orchestra. It was a huge concert—the stage was lit from behind with a silhouette of the New York skyline, and I couldn't believe how many people were in the audience. The orchestra's dress code was "glam black": tuxedos for men, long black gowns for women. I was so, so excited to join my teachers, Levine and Fran Andrade, onstage.

I was only seventeen, and the day of the concert, I had traveled to the venue in sparkly silver ballet flats and normal streetwear, saving my black shoes and dress for the concert. When I changed into my dress right before the show, I didn't notice beneath my floor-length skirt that I had left those sparkly silver glitter shoes on until I was standing in the stage wings, moments away from the start of the concert. Fran was waiting nearby. "I've messed up!" I told her. "I left my shoes backstage! I'm wearing silver!" I was terrified—the wrong shoes, what an embarrassing mistake! Fran looked at me and laughed with the best smile any teacher could ever give a student. "The dress code is *glam* black, dahhling, and those silver shoes are certainly glam!" With that, we walked onstage together.

Many mentors understand the importance of maintaining high performance standards, but few have the presence of mind in moments of crisis to also preserve a budding musician's self-confidence. Fran recognized there was no way for me to change my shoes. Calling further attention to my error would only have diminished my focus onstage. The best creative mentors balance their high standards with a healthy perspective of what is truly important for children to hear at any given moment.

## Fitting Creativity into Boundaries

Creativity is wonderful, but part of being a creative person is knowing where and when to "play the game" instead. For example, if an English teacher wants an essay on a specific topic that goes over specific points, students have to learn how to tailor their creativity to match the assignment. Treat this as an additional creative challenge—"Hey, I know you want to compose a new piece—that's wonderful! Your teacher wants you to compose a fugue, specifically. Can you follow their instructions exactly?" In this way, a child's creativity isn't hampered or treated negatively. It's just redirected to fit a specific goal.

## Other Subjects

For every family that adds music to a long list of extracurricular activities, there's another family worried that pursuing music will detract from attaining excellence in core subjects. As a music teacher, I'm not in a position to tell families the best academic path—which subjects to pursue and which to drop as a student matures. However, I can say this: as long a child is sleeping enough, eating healthfully, attending classes regularly, and taking time to relax with friends and family, extracurricular activities that seem to compete (for time each day) with music only help children grow into efficient learners who excel at different types of learning. For example, language teaches students to listen to nuance. Ballet teaches students to respond to that nuance in movement. Team sports teach collaboration. Girl Scouts and Boy Scouts facilitate development in multiple ways, especially as a result of following the procedures required on projects to earn advanced badges. Until the middle school homework begins to pile up, embracing multiple avenues of study helps children become adept at different types of learning. Critically, the pursuit of new endeavors helps everyone understand that it's okay—and fun!—to be a beginner in any subject.

Part of being creative is understanding what it feels like to be new at something—there's an inherent vulnerability in all creative arts. When your child can recall being new at dance, music, language, and other subjects, it helps them—later in life—summon an invaluable appreciation for any project in its early stages. Creative work doesn't have to immediately demonstrate value to the world, it only has to bring joy to its creator.

---

### Other Instruments

*"But, Mommmm, I really want to be a drummer! I hate violin! I'M SO BORED."*

There's a belief that if a young musician is going to be truly skilled, they should perform on only one instrument. However, if your child is eager to play in a band with their friends, let them. As long as the primary instrument is practiced daily, gravitating toward another instrument should not be frowned upon. Avoid implying that the second instrument or genre is less worthwhile than the first one. Celebrate the diversity your child brings to your family's appreciation for the arts. Congratulations, you have a child who is expanding their—and your—horizons!

---

## Fear and Anxiety

Fear and anxiety are the biggest enemies of musical proficiency and artistry. Fear of failure (truly, an anxiety over "not being good enough") often disguises itself as a scheduling problem. As adults, we rationalize that the real reason we never ran that marathon, took up painting, or mastered the flute is that we just never had the time. Anxiety loves excuses, and it's exceptionally good at generating them. After all, if we have a reasonable excuse for why we didn't do the requisite work to attain excellence in a field, no one can hold our mediocrity against us, right? Like adults, children are susceptible to letting these feelings distract them from achieving their musical goals. Also like adults, children have a difficult time recognizing anxieties for what they really are.

Procrastination, then, should be viewed as the habit of choosing a friendly ideal situation for today—"I'll just practice more tomorrow, I still have time to do well!"—instead of engaging with musical work and the anxieties surrounding it. Procrastination may be a comfortable choice in the short term, but it creates misery in the long run. When goals ultimately come up short, the resulting disappointment confirms procrastinators' fears about their own abilities. Failures like this, of course, do not make children more likely to start the next project earlier, as their parents might hope. Instead, these failures just contribute to a cycle of fear, procrastination, and disappointment.

Kids aren't always able to connect these dots between procrastination and anxiety, let alone articulate this issue to parents and teachers. That makes anxiety a much trickier thing to identify and confront. So, how do we help children get around it?

## Habit

The first way to tackle fear and anxiety is to make our most meaningful and important tasks an unchangeable part of our daily routine. If practicing at the same time each day is a solid habit, it's a lot harder to find excuses to skip out of that daily work, even when fear sneaks in to undermine self-confidence. When children feel they don't have enough time to work on their biggest musical goals, it's often just that they're overwhelmed, anxious about the many tasks at hand. Turn musical work into a scheduled, predictable, reliable habit and, instead of thinking or worrying about practicing, kids just practice. Think of it this way: there's no need for kids to agonize every morning about whether to brush their teeth once it's a strong habit—they just follow through with it. By removing the question of when to practice, young musicians and their parents can eliminate the time spent worrying about it and get right down to work. This defeats dread before it creeps in and allows children to focus directly on accomplishing their musical tasks.

## Hope

Why would anyone ever commit time to beginning a project sooner than absolutely necessary if they thought the jump start might not actually benefit them in the long run? Practicing is intimidating, and children, especially beginners, don't always perceive how effective practicing truly is. I tell my students, "Talent will strike, but it has to find you practicing." Young musicians need to enter the practice room with the firm conviction that no matter what, they will move forward through their efforts. With that reassurance, they can put forth wholehearted effort. The affirmation of guaranteed progress validates every effort.

Parents can help by noticing and encouraging this behavior. On top of that, look for ways to remind children that the true measure of their own initiative level is not the practicing for which they get credit from their parents and teachers, but the practicing they choose to do when no one is even around to hear them. When children truly believe in their musical potential, they gravitate toward the instrument, motivated by their progress and hopeful for their musical future. Without an unshakeable belief in their own ability to generate progress, a child is more likely to choose a truly passive activity over practicing.

---

## The Power of Positive Phrases

Children can't expect a life free of nerves—learning just has too many big challenges in store. Instead, help your child realize that no matter what the scary obstacle today is, they can effectively prepare in advance to decide how to react.

Frame upcoming experiences with positive language. Having your child repeat, "I won't get nervous" will lead them to Nerves Central. Musicians' bodies and brains focus on the negative word "nervous" regardless of the "won't." Instead, teach your child to repeat positive phrases like, "I'll keep my eyes on my fingers. I'll play well—I know it." That will direct their focus to the task at hand.

---

## Stage Fright

It's a familiar frustration: after all of that effort in the practice room and all the energy spent on lessons, a young musician's performance falls apart on stage as a result of nerves. To develop your child's confidence in performance situations as they mature, have them perform frequently at home and around town from the earliest age possible. Encourage them to perform for a variety of audiences, including hospitals, nursing homes, parties, recitals, competitions, chair tests, and auditions. Consistent and positive performance experiences in new situations will help your child learn to enjoy performing as they grow.

## Feeling Intimidated

Stage fright's favorite colleague is intimidation. Musicians walk into grand concert halls, unfamiliar and awe-inspiring environments, and are introduced to important individuals they have been told will hold sway over their musical future. Of course that's intimidating!

Parents and educators can help children perform at their best even when they feel intimidated by reminding young musicians that everyone starts out as a beginner. If children go to an audition and feel like they don't belong, that's okay. They are there first and foremost to put forth their best effort and walk away with a new experience.

Dealing with nerves is challenging because it changes how children feel physically during performances. Their shoulders climb up, their hands shake, and musical gestures fall flat. Students tell me, "I played this perfectly at home, I just can't do it here—I'm nervous because you're listening!" That feeling is relatable, but it's one of the realities musicians face: performing means playing in front of people. As a teacher, I can't change that fact. Instead, I encourage students to keep pushing through anyway—anyone can learn to manage nerves as long as they are willing to keep working.

That brings me to one of my violin students, Tammy. Tammy had advanced to the second round of an audition a year earlier than most students do. When she heard the other advancing players perform, she found them to all be older than her, with bigger instruments and better sound. She was worried the judges had made some mistake—surely, she didn't belong there, and she was taking up another violinist's spot! She confided this in her orchestra director, who was shocked to hear Tammy felt this way. Tammy did absolutely deserve to be in this next round! Tammy's director knew that sometimes we all feel like we accidentally got into the VIP room. This is just a part of learning to accurately assess one's own strengths and weaknesses! The key is to not let that inner voice of doubt prevent one from embracing each new opportunity.

It takes a lot of guts to play confidently. It takes self-assurance for a child to move the bow purposefully on the string, put practicing into their schedule each day, and know that their work will pay off. It takes true bravery to be willing to risk missing notes in front of others and freely express musical and artistic ideas in front of a group. Remind your child that this effort doesn't go unnoticed. Even those big, confident kids in advanced orchestras had to go through it to get to where they are.

---

### Adam's Concert

One way to help children overcome their fear of a new task (for example, performing on an instrument for the first time) is to complement it with one of their strengths. For example, when one of my students, Adam, was five, he was ready to give his recital debut. He would be playing a few short rhythms on the violin's open strings. Each rhythm had a name: Pepperoni Pizza, Ice-Cream Shh Cone, Pony, Gotta Get a Motorcycle, and Spider-Man. Adam was nervous about his first performance, so we decided he would do what he thought he did best: tell the audience a story right before he began to play the violin. At five, Adam loved making up stories and capturing an audience's attention, even though he was nervous about that same room full of people watching him play violin.

"Once upon a time," he started, "I was really hungry, so I wanted to have some Pepperoni Pizza. Then, my teacher said I could have an Ice-Cream Shh Cone! We went on an adventure with a Pony, but then I said I've Gotta Get a Motorcycle because it would go faster. THEN, to go even faster, I went flying with Spider-Man!" Adam received huge applause for his story, and, now encouraged, he was ready to perform his rhythms. We had turned something intimidating—a first recital—into a chance for Adam to shine.

---

## Reject Fear When It's Used as a Teaching Tactic

Good fear involves anticipation—new experiences that help one grow. Bad fear is fear that gets in the way of learning and can be paralyzing. When a child is excited or nervous to meet a new teacher or perform, they feel good fear. When a teacher shouts or a child feels unprepared onstage, the child experiences bad fear. Parents and teachers can show children how to manage both types of fear. We empower students when we allow good-fear experiences. We hurt them when we see bad-fear situations and don't provide the best available solution.

For example, many private teachers and orchestra instructors use fear purposefully as a teaching tactic. "Old-school" pedagogy tradition is sometimes represented by a perfectionist teacher who throws objects and screams no matter how well the student is doing, in an effort to push them to try harder.

However, I believe today's scientific research about how the brain handles fear. Teaching through fear is often counterproductive and, in many cases, downright destructive. When students are terrified, their brains shut down higher-level learning and memory. They default to an emotional, fight-or-flight state. This state of mind cannot facilitate the accurate finger movements that performances (often involving thousands of nuanced notes) require.

My own former teachers—whose help I have been enormously grateful for over the years—have told me that they were aggressively preparing me for the outside world and for critics. "I'm on your side," one teacher told me. "But I'm preparing you for the people who won't be." That rational, honest criticism enabled me to analyze my playing the way a critic might. However, that line is also often used by teachers to justify behaviors that should not be allowed in the learning environment.

It's one thing to prepare a student for reviews from critics. It's another to verbally abuse them, throw objects, make threats, or bully them into practicing. Motivation by fear cannot lead to sustainable self-motivation. The minute the teacher and the fear are removed from the equation, no further progress will be demonstrated because a truly self-motivated student has not been developed. As a parent, take protective action and remove your child from situations where abusive teaching is present.

## Quitting: Fear's Greatest Victory

When a child feels overwhelmed, the short-term urge to quit (in response to stress) sometimes outweighs the long-term desire to play music. You can help your child through the toughest challenges to help them stay on track to enjoy playing music for life. Here are some examples of struggles that seem earth-shattering to children but can certainly be overcome with proper guidance from parents and teachers.

*"The music is too hard."* If difficult music has been assigned, it's a sign that your child's teacher believes in their potential and is ready to help them get there faster. Ask your child or their teacher to break down the music into planned, manageable chunks—one line per day, or even (for the most difficult passages) ten minutes per measure. This gives children a chance to conquer the music through repetition. Ten minutes is nothing in the long run, but it goes far in transforming an intimidating passage from impossible to playable. Every time we show children that this transformation is possible, we give them the tools they need to conquer difficult material in the future as well.

*"All of my friends have quit orchestra."* If playing music were easy, everyone would do it. It's okay for your child to watch their friends quit. It means that what your child is doing is extraordinary. Find

189

additional social opportunities for your child, and remind them that some challenges might force other players to give up, but the two of you are ready to tackle these things and succeed.

*"I won't be ready for the audition. I have too much other work to do."* Young musicians won't always tell a parent when they have been neglecting their musical assignments and are now behind on their pre-audition progress. What parents will see is that about three weeks before a big audition, children suddenly feel overwhelmed—they want to quit. Many children miscalculate their planning like this, but it's better to learn that lesson (whether or not they follow through with the audition) than it is to just quit to avoid the short-term failure of a rough audition. Don't let a short-term change of plans lead to a life without music.

*"It's just not as much fun as it used to be."* No matter how much one loves the material, at some point any subject will involve true work. Remind your child that something doesn't have to be fun 24/7 for it to be worthwhile. Phases truly are just phases. See what you can do to make the work more fun (join a new orchestra, start some new repertoire) and agree to reassess in a few months.

*"I don't have the time."* When children feel like they don't have enough time, it's often that their scheduling routine needs to be adjusted to allow for homework and practicing deadlines. When practicing is part of a routine, it doesn't add to the feeling of being overwhelmed.

*"I'm not as good as Sally."* Remind your child that the mere presence of another skilled musician is not a valid reason to quit. Sally won't be at every performance your child will ever give. Sally certainly won't be around when your child is applying to college. For all we know, Sally might well move to Montana next year. As a strategy, tell your child that your family doesn't base life or academic decisions based on Sally's existence, no matter how talented Sally is. The world

will always have talented people, and with several billion of us on the planet, there will always be someone more skilled and someone less skilled than your child. That doesn't mean their work is invalid, redundant, or anything less than completely necessary.

*"My teacher doesn't like me."* That's okay. A teacher doesn't have to make the student feel liked—some teachers do a poor job of conveying that they like their students, but that fact doesn't justify quitting. It may justify changing studios, but quitting music is just too damaging to allow a lousy teacher to cause it. Assure your child that they will have different types of teachers as they grow up—some will like them and some might not seem to. When it's not in your power as the parent to change teachers, treat this as a learning experience. We all have to deal with people in authority positions whether they like us personally or not. As long as the teacher is not abusive in any way, this is an opportunity to teach your child about relationship management as it applies to their mentors.

*"But I don't want to be a musician when I grow up."* Here's your answer: "This isn't about whether or not you become a musician. This is about keeping doors open to any career or hobby you might someday like to pursue. Playing an instrument builds musical skills, academic skills, and soft skills. For your own future happiness, I would like you to grow up with the advantages all of these traits will bring you."

*"But I can't do it."* Kids grow. Abilities develop. Sticking with music allows students the chance to experience this skill development and find out for themselves that they really can learn things that start out as "impossible."

*"But I didn't get the audition results I wanted. I failed."* When an adult adjudicator gives a child undesirable feedback, whether accurate or not, the child sometimes feels hopeless—like their work was wasted. This is especially true when the child feels that the

competition results were somehow unfair. Remind your child to take the good with the bad and not let a perfect stranger (the adjudicator in the audition) determine whether they will have music in their life. In a year, this audition will seem far away. What will matter then is your child's understanding of their own progress.

## Heartfelt Creativity

*"Today, Ben told me, 'Mom, no matter what it takes, I will learn to play The Swan. It's tricky and it might take me a few weeks, but I love every note and I know I can do it.'"*

*Celine, mother of eight-year-old Ben*

Heartfelt creativity is the defiance of self-doubt in the pursuit of bringing music, art, and ideas into the world. To develop it in your child, champion the critical thinking skills that lead to self-directed progress. Look for chances to connect with others through art, whether that art is familiar or completely new to your family. Show the value of learning the "rules" present in any discipline. Build on that field-specific knowledge by teaching the complementary skill of thinking outside the box, inspiring your child to call on their own expertise and experience to bring new ideas into existence.

No person, regardless of credentials, is more innately talented than or superior to your child. Your child has the only thing that truly matters in their pursuit of motivation and talent: you. As their parent, you are the most important teacher they will ever have. No Beethoven, Einstein, or Picasso could teach them more than you can. Every note, technique, essay, science project, and performance you tackle together presents the opportunity for your child to develop meaningful learning skills that will guide them through their life's adventures.

# Afterword

"DAD, I WANT to play violin."

Just before my fifth birthday, my parents took me to see a high school orchestra perform Prokofiev's *Peter & the Wolf*. Looking up at the big stage, I fell completely in love with the violin. At first, my well-meaning parents tried to talk me out of it. Hoping to avoid listening to a small child learn the world's squeakiest instrument, they even bought me a cello.

I begged for a violin. My parents relented, and gave me a violin so tiny it wouldn't have looked out of place hanging on a Christmas tree. They presented the snubbed cello to my younger brother with great flair. "See, Nathan, now you can play just like Lauren!"

As itty-bitty musicians playing pieces like "Pepperoni Pizza" at the Minnesota Valley Music School, my brother and I had no idea how much music would shape our lives. In true illustration of this, my brother goes by "Cello." The name fits.

My favorite family photo shows my parents, brother, and me practicing together at home in the early '90s. In it, my mother sits at the piano, looking over at my father. My father holds his own cello (procured to help my brother). It has brightly colored tapes all over the fingerboard. Nathan sits on a tiny yellow "cello chair" with his instrument and I'm playing my violin. My bow-hold looks good, but one sock is halfway off. Everyone is smiling.

Whenever I hear families wonder aloud if they have what it takes to develop musical motivation and talent, I show them that photo to illustrate how my musical journey started.

Just like theirs.

# Suggested Resources

Covey, Sean. *The 7 Habits of Highly Effective Teens*. New York: Touchstone, 2014.

Covey, Stephen. *The 7 Habits of Highly Successful People: Powerful Lessons in Personal Change*. New York: Simon & Schuster, 2013.

Gilbert, Elizabeth. *Big Magic: Creative Living Beyond Fear*. New York: Riverhead Books, 2016.

Pausch, Randy. *The Last Lecture*. With Jeffrey Zaslow. New York: Hyperion, 2008.

Salerno-Sonnenberg, Nadja. *Nadja On My Way*. New York: Knopf Books for Young Readers, 1989.

Steinhardt, Arnold. *Violin Dreams*. New York: Houghton Mifflin Harcourt, 2006.

Steinhardt, Arnold. *Indivisible by Four: A String Quartet in Pursuit of Harmony*. New York: Farrar, Straus and Giroux, 2000.

Suzuki, Shinichi. *Nurtured by Love*. Los Angeles: Alfred Music, 1986.

# Acknowledgments

WITH GRATITUDE AND love to my parents, Jim and Lisa Haley, for their guidance, patience, and encouragement from "Twinkle" to Tchaikovsky. Thanks to Nathaniel "Cello" Haley, my favorite (and only) brother.

Thank you to Albertine Wang, writer/photographer/pianist/ design extraordinaire. Albertine, you truly are a Swiss Army knife of the creative arts.

With heartfelt appreciation to my own violin teachers—I think of you all every day. Thank you.

In loving memory of Fran Andrade, Fredell Lack, and Zvi Zeitlin.

With many thanks to Ruth and Russell Peck, whose enthusiasm for teaching shaped my own.

Köszönöm szépen, Dama, for a life in music.

Thank you to Vicki Tashjian for believing in this book from start to finish.

To my students and the LHS families—I am so thrilled to work with you each day.

Huge thanks to Jenn, Niki, Karen, Lisa, and the whole PDP team.

With love to my husband, Jake Baumler.

# About the Author

LAUREN ALEXANDRA HALEY is a professional violinist, violist, and music educator based in Houston, Texas. Haley earned a degree in Violin Performance from the Eastman School of Music in Rochester, New York. Accepted into both the violin and viola performance programs at Eastman, she studied with Oleh Krysa, Phillip Ying, and Zvi Zeitlin.

An educational entrepreneur, Haley is the Founder of Lauren Haley Studios, where she enrolls over 50 young musicians studying violin and viola. Lauren Haley Studios is known for transforming beginning orchestra students into section leaders. Haley's students routinely win awards and honors at local events, give volunteer community performances, and serve as concertmasters and principal players at their schools.

Haley performs on a 1750's Thomas Smith violin, a 1930's Francois Lotte bow, and a modern viola.

77294436R00121

Made in the USA
Middletown, DE
20 June 2018